Living in the
NAMES OF GOD
HIS MAJESTY AND ME

What Others Are Saying

I just finished your book, His Majesty in Brokenness. *Thank you for your openness, for exposing your brokenness, and for making the effort to write for us. Thank you for letting Abba God use you in so many ways.*

Amy Mayfield

Thank you for sharing your life in your book. Your "What about You?" section at the end of each chapter is very penetrating, bold and helpful. Thank you for your honesty and humor in telling your story.

Marge Perry

Judy, your sharing how Jesus met you in your different struggles was so encouraging. I liked your format of asking the reader for his or her personal application; this made it like an interactive Bible study. I also loved how you connected the dots of biblical precepts to scripture and to real life situations.

Pam Koning

Even though I got your book only yesterday, it's already speaking to me big time! One of my favorite parts is how you talk about the fact that pain is inevitable in life and everyone relates to disability in one form or another. I believe this book is going to speak to people in a more powerful and impacting way than you can even imagine. Thank you for this masterpiece you have created. Your book is a brilliant gem.

Ben Courson

I shared your book with a friend who was just diagnosed with breast cancer. She took it with her to her appointment today and held it in her hand the whole time the doctors were giving her the treatment plan. She said it's the kind of book she needs to read right now, especially the "What about You?" part.

Martha Rippere

My words fall so short of expressing what a healing gift your book, your stories, your life have been to me! Each chapter was so healing to my weary soul. Brokenness is JUST what the Lord has been teaching me about these past few years. There's no denying that beauty lives there, healing lives there, intimacy lives there and life lives there. It's not what I necessarily want to experience, so to hear your stories chapter after chapter, gave me courage to keep walking this path of Christ's strength in my weakness.

Jenny Fitzgerald

Living in the
NAMES OF GOD

HIS MAJESTY AND ME

JUDY SQUIER

Self-published by Judy Squier.
www.judysquier.com

Cover & interior design by Naphtalie Joiner (www.scatterjoydesigns.com)
Cover photo & author photo by Naphtalie Joiner (www.scatterjoyphotos.com)

Disclaimer: At the onset, may I beg your scholastic mercy. These stories are not
intended for microscopic examination by theological scholars but they are intended
to convey an attainable-to-all relationship with the God of the Universe.

Squier, Judy
Living in the Names of God / by Judy Squier
                ISBN-10: 1491029188
                ISBN-13: 978-1491029183

Printed in the United States of America

Dedicated to El Shaddai,
The God who has met me, a woman
born with incomplete legs, at every stage of life.
Truly You have wooed me with Your love
and wowed me with Your might.

Contents

In Appreciation

Thank you to David, my husband extraordinaire,
who sacrificially provides his love,
his legs and his brains to keep me moving forward.

Thank you to Naphy Joy,
my graphic artist daughter, whose design skills
and cheers carried this book to the finish line.

Thank you, Kay Arthur,
for being the first to teach me about living
life in God's holy names.

Thank you to three pastors –
Bob Bonner, Don Needham and Dean Smith –
for teaching me that God's many names
match my many needs.

Thank you to my Calvary Crossroads Bible class,
my guinea pigs, who read and studied the chapters
as I wrote them.

Thank you to two prayer warriors, cousin Sue and Marcia
and a special thank you to my pal Ginny
and her husband Dallas for reading,
critiquing and praying for each chapter.

And a special thank you to the many readers
of my first book, *His Majesty in Brokenness*.
Knowing that my God-stories brought you
strength for the journey gave me the strength needed
to write this book you hold in your hands.

BEFORE YOU BEGIN

My friend Judy Squier may be one of God's best friends – she knows His name well and spreads the fame of His name to everyone she meets. She has tapped into the power of God's name time and again and has proved that name true and faithful.

I first met Judy back in the 1980s when I spoke at her church in the Bay Area... her winsome smile bolstered my spirits, especially when I noticed that she was walking on prosthetic legs. *I want to know this woman!* I remember thinking. And through the years, through the many times we connected at Joni and Friends' Family Retreats and other events, I have been blessed by her hopeful outlook and great sense of humor. Where does she get that winning attitude? Simply from knowing God. So it's no surprise that Judy Squier would write about the glorious name of God in this unique and personal book.

Why write about the names of God? Well, it is doubtful that any phrase in our prayer vocabulary is voiced more frequently -- and understood less -- than the three-word expression "In Jesus' name." Yet our capacity to trust the Lord is clearly linked to our knowledge of God's name. Shakespeare once asked, "What is in a name? A rose by any other name would smell as sweet." Thankfully in this book, Judy tackles Shakespeare's question, helping us understand exactly what is in the name of God.

As you will learn in *Living in the Names of God,* there are so many aspects of our Christian life that are connected to His name. The psalmist said, "Those who know your name will put their trust in You" (Psalm 9:10). And when we battle our adversary, our victory is intimately linked to the name of the Lord, "Through your name we will trample those who rise up against us" (Psalm 44:5).

So, living in and praying in God's name means much more than merely voicing a three-word expression at the close of a prayer. To live in the name of our Savior means to step into each new day in the power of His grace and glory. Each of His names in His Word reflects a special characteristic, a unique attribute of who He is... and the study of these names grants us personal access to His mighty strength.

Judy Squier has certainly needed that strength through the years. Walking through life with no legs? That's quite a feat! But her disability has never given her an excuse to sin or slander the name of God through bitter disappointment. Rather than stain God's good reputation, Judy has used her disability as a springboard into a deeper and sweeter union with Jesus Christ. And it has been through abiding in Jesus and His Word that my friend has become intimately acquainted with His name.

The book you hold in your hands is like a journal of her lively and buoyant relationship with the God of the universe. It is like a diary that details her devotion for God's various names. It is my prayer that as you read her stories – as well as the stories she shares about her precious Lord – you, too, will learn to lean on the great and glorious name of God!

© Joni Eareckson Tada
Joni and Friends International Disability Center
Spring 2013

יהוה יהוה יהוה יהוה יהוה יהוה יהוה יהוה יהוה
Our help is in the name of the Lord.
Psalm 124:8a (NASB)

ELOHIM
Mighty Creator

EL GIBBOR
Mighty Warrior

EL ELYON
The Most High God

JEHOVAH JIREH
The Lord Will Provide

JEHOVAH
I AM WHO I AM

ADONAI
Lord and Master

JEHOVAH RAAH
The Lord My Shepherd

ADONAI TSURI
The Lord My Rock

The Names of God

JEHOVAH SHAMMAH
The Lord is There

JEHOVAH RAPHA
The Lord Who Heals

EL ROI
The God Who Sees

JEHOVAH SHALOM
The Lord is Peace

JEHOVAH NISSI
The Lord is My Banner

JEHOVAH MEKODDISHKEM
The Lord Who Sanctifies

JEHOVAH TSIDKENU
The Lord Our Righteousness

EL OLAM
The Everlasting God

GO'EL
God My Redeemer

EL SHADDAI
The All-Sufficient God

Psalm 124:8a (NASB)
Our help is in the name of the Lord.
יהוה יהוה יהוה יהוה יהוה יהוה יהוה יהוה יהוה

1

His Majesty and Me

HOW MY LOVE AFFAIR BEGAN

I will forever remember the Saturday morning in autumn that began with a loud crash followed by an agonizing ouch. You ask me, "Judy, what hurt?"

Actually, my husband David was the one who was hurting when he and his roaring chainsaw fell fifteen feet off a ladder onto our driveway's blacktop. Come to find out his anklebone was shattered into seventy pieces while doing my honey-do list. His words to the ER nurse who greeted the ambulance were: "You have to save my leg; my wife has none." She dismissed it as delirium.

David's accident knocked me off my feet, or more accurately, knocked me off my stumps. Weren't his legs mine too? Didn't I, a double amputee walking on artificial limbs, rely on his strong legs for parenting our three children and for balancing our busy household?

That was the year David and I tied for the World's Most Helpless title as my ordered life toppled during his two-week hospitalization, three surgeries and months of recovery. I changed my name from Judy to Job as one thing after another went kaput. First David's leg, *then* the transmission problems on my specially-adapted minivan. *Then* a broken oven which no repairman could fix with Thanksgiving only three weeks away. *Then* the worst case of bark beetle the local arborist had ever seen infesting our thirteen sky high Monterey pines. *Plus* – not good timing – the accident came two days before a mega-remodel on our home was to begin. And, oh, I'd just begun my first term as co-president of our daughters' school's PTA.

Unable to get beyond the robotical performance of the necessities, I squeezed out, "God, this is way too BIG! I'll take all the help You can muster. Send the troops." Enter Kay Arthur's book, *Lord, I Want to Know You,* a devotional study of the names of God.[1] First I met *El Shaddai,* who promised to replace my too little with His so big. His strength met my weakness and carried me across each day's finish line.

Everyone I encountered – doctors for my husband and doctors for trees, construction workers at our home, the auto and appliance repairmen – heard my daily accounts of a God Who Cares About Every Detail of Our Lives. No one asked questions when a hope-bearing name plaque inscribed with *El Shaddai* replaced a battle weary *Squiers* above the front door.

Along with *El Shaddai,* other Hebrew names of God became household words. *El Elyon,* the Most High God, was my newfound power source who carried me on His shoulders. *Jehovah Raah* (Raah! Raah!) became my Shepherd Cheerleader. *Jehovah Jireh,* the God Who Provides, was true to His word, as He more than provided for our family's daily needs. God faithfully came to my rescue and downed my giants with a single blow.

Thanks to David's blessed accident, God showed up on my doorstep.

Judy and temporarily disabled husband David

(Actually, He was always there, but I missed seeing Him because I believed the myth that I could handle life on my own.) His troops consisted of eighteen Hebrew names of God, which having met men of old at their point of need now kept their promise to meet me.

No longer just a concept, God became a living presence, a family member, my constant companion every step of the way. What Tim Hansel explains in his book, *You Gotta Keep Dancing,* describes what happened to me. "The goal in this life we call Christian is that all of our theology become biography."[2] Most definitely the God of my theology intercepted my life and entered my biography. My cry for help was heard by our Almighty God who showed up with His troops and more.

Living in the names of God, what does it look like? My four-year-old granddaughter Brianna provided the answer one morning while her mom was driving her to preschool.

Out of the blue, Brianna asked,
"Mom, Where is God?"
"In heaven," her mom answered.
"No, He's sitting in the car
right next to you," Brianna said.
"Hi God, how are You?" her mom replied.
To which Brianna commented,
"He says He loves you."

What About You?

Are you ready for your theology to become biography? Are you ready to put a face with God's name? Maybe you view theology as something for those religious folk. You just want to mind your own business. But what if there's Someone who offers – free of charge – to make your business His business, because He made you and He's the only One who can make life work? Getting up close and personal, He longs to companion with you every step of life's way.

He holds the answers, because He is the answer;
He loves you on good days and bad; no strings attached;
He's even capable of making you into the person
you've always wanted to be, because He's your Creator;

His approval never fluctuates;
Your worth is no longer based
on what you do but what He did for you;
In Him your potential exceeds each day's demands;
He promises to make right all your wrongs;

He can even pull off making pain
and suffering not just worthwhile
but the best thing that happened to you;
He'll never write you off but promises to be your BFF –
Best Friend Forever.

That's the God who showed up on my radar screen that autumn in the early 1990s. Knowing His many names enabled me to see His capable presence – ready, willing and able to meet my every need. Plus, knowing Him more intimately freed me daily to face my every weakness. Didn't He promise to love me no matter what? Didn't He have the power to make me soar?

Oh, how I long for you, dear reader, to know Him too – to know His love when love is nowhere to be found, to know His approval when all you hear is condemnation, to know His power when you're paralyzed by powerlessness, and to know His peace that comforts and brings purpose to every storm.

May the following chapters provide for you a life-changing encounter with the God whose names not only help you understand who He is, but help you understand who you are. As you answer yes to His invitation to be in relationship with Him, I pray His names intercept your life as they did mine so you can see Him co-starring in your story. His Majesty and you. You're a team.

2

Elohim

MIGHTY CREATOR

The Creator God Who Makes No Mistakes

Is it possible that even Creator God cringed the midnight of my birth? Not because my deformities repulsed Him. Never! In His eyes, my body was perfect, defects and all. No, He wouldn't cringe beholding His *fearfully and wonderfully* made creation, but is it possible He cringed at the obstetrician's revulsion as my birth defect and I slipped through the birth canal?

In the doctor's defense, he had no warning. Hospitals had no ultrasound machines in the 1940s. He was totally unprepared to meet the newborn who arrived with a sorrowful excuse for legs: no thighs or knees, only twig-like extensions ending with two contorted feet – three toes on the left and two on the right. Plus, there was a webbed left hand – *that* was almost missed.

Surely the delivery room doc was dumbstruck. What should he tell the parents? Mom was still under the effects of the anesthesia; she could wait. But Dad was in the waiting room and had to be told. Stumbling through the door and struggling to compose himself, the doctor simply blurted out: "Reverend Rieder, your daughter is going to live, I'm sorry to say."

That was Dad's recollection. He told the story many times. Talking about it seemed to reduce his pain. But he never told what happened next. Did he break down in tears? Did he burst into questions? Did he go see for himself?

I do know it was Sunday and he had a sermon to preach. Only God remembers the sermon topic that hardest morning of my Dad's life. John 9:1-12 would have been apropos. To hear *Elohim* the Creator God's view about birth defects would have benefitted the congregation, but most of all the preacher. His disciples asked Him, saying, *"Rabbi, who sinned, this man or his parents that he should be born blind?" Jesus answered, "It was neither that this man sinned, nor his parents, but it was in order that the works of God might be displayed in him."* (John 9:2-3 NASB)

Like the blind man's father and mother, I'm sure Dad and Mom would have experienced a mega-dose of relief to hear Jesus' words: *"You're asking the wrong question. You're looking for someone to blame. There is no such cause-effect here. Look instead for what God can do."* (John 9:3 MSG)

For any family reeling from the news of their just-born-baby's birth defect, Jesus' words would eliminate blame and redirect the focus to God's upcoming masterpiece. Oh the joy when guilt is buried and hope is born and we can say: *You mean it's not our fault? You mean God is in it? Are you telling us something good can come out of this? You aren't kidding- God will be on display in this? You promise? Elohim,* the Creator of all things, answers yes to all the above. He's there to comfort and carry us through life's shockers.

Back at the hospital Mom smelled trouble the minute she woke from the anesthesia. How often does a mother have to wait three days before meeting her baby? Yet she tells that my arrival into her room brought a smile amidst the devastation as she watched me turn over in the nurse's nervous arms. A ray of hope was born the minute she detected spunk.

I'm told church elders were the only ones brave enough to come visit once we were home. Strange, they didn't even ask to see the new baby. They had come for only one reason – to tell my father that surely his sin had brought on such a calamity. How did Dad respond to that message? He never told us how he felt. Our family was stoic and did not talk about feelings.

Heaven heard no praise from the Rieder family that cold winter in upstate New York. But weren't my parents Christians? Yes, Dad was a minister and Mom was a minister's wife and the daughter of Bishop Epp. It was easy to conclude that heaven had turned a deaf ear to their unspoken plea – the prayer of every parent's heart: "All we want, God, is a healthy baby."

What does a body do when hearts are bleeding and dreams are crushed? Truth be told, the road to God's comfort can be long and circuitous. Come to find out tears are acceptable for people of faith; doubts don't surprise God, nor do clenched fists. His love woos us as He waits patiently for us to be able to accept His embrace.

God's embrace is ever available to us through others, circumstances, and through His Word, the Bible. I stand amazed that I didn't learn about Psalm 139 until I was twenty years old. God bless the saint who finally introduced me to the truths about Creator God's holy design for each one of us:

You made all the delicate,
inner parts of my body and
knit me together in my mother's womb.
Thank you for making me
so wonderfully complex!
Your workmanship is marvelous—
and how well I know it.
You were there while I was being
formed in utter seclusion!
You saw me before I was born
and scheduled each
day of my life before I began to breathe.
Every day was recorded in your Book!
(Psalm 139:13-16 TLB)

The day I realized that Creator God was on duty in utero – initiating, skillfully crafting, and sovereignly planning – was the day I grew dancing legs. I know now that no matter how bad it looks or feels, *Elohim's* design is flawless. His work bears the stamp: No Fetal Flukes, All Holy Design.

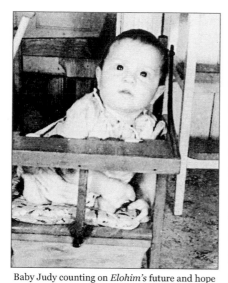
Baby Judy counting on *Elohim's* future and hope

The verses from Psalm 139 have provided a firm foundation for me to stand on during inevitable struggles to accept *Elohim's* perfect design for my imperfect body. Accepting *Elohim's* design can be a lifelong quest. It was for my family. It has been for me. What a stretch to believe that suffering can bring forth blessings when it hurts so bad.

Dad would recount how bad it hurt by telling how he and Mom sat along the shore of Geneva, New York's Lake Seneca during the first year of my life. Playing in the sand was their three-year-old daughter, Tina – how long and strong were her legs. Between them was a wicker basket containing broken me.

Dad never hid the fact that his fists shook heavenward that day as he thundered, "What do you have in mind, God, for our Judy Ann?" The stormy, white-capped lake, like the storm raging inside of him, drowned out the still, small voice whispering on my behalf: *"Trust Me. For I know the plans I have for her,"* says the LORD. *"They are plans for good and not for disaster, to give her a future and a hope."* (Author's

paraphrase of Jeremiah 29:11 NLT)

Fast-forward almost seven decades. Mom and Dad are safely Home. It all makes sense for them now. My sister Tina and I are finally processing all the pieces. Our favorite pastime is reminiscing about the early years we shared together. We talk about how she felt as she stood outside my window at Shriners Hospital when only the parents could visit for three hours on Sundays. We discuss the pain we both felt when other kids and even their parents gawked at me; it amazes me every time she tells how she saw in my lonely life something that her full life lacked. We both conclude, she saw *Someone* – the One who companions with those who hurt and are left out.

Aunt Ruth's wise proverb

We all hurt back then but never talked about it. Life's pain felt like it would never end. But it did. And now we know what God knew all along – Broken Judy would become a display case for His glory just like Jesus promised in John 9.

Despite all the truth that I have learned about *Elohim's* perfect design and plan for my life, my birthday week has for decades been a downer. March 3rd, the day before my birthday, became a wear-black day as I would grieve the pain my disability and I brought to my parents. The Good Lord companions with us in our suffering, and in His perfect time provides understanding and healing.

I still smile to think how He used our now grown daughter, Elizabeth, to retire my wear-black, doomsday uniform and set me free. Catching wind of my March 3, 2011 burdened heart, she pondered my pain throughout the day as she busied herself with her two-year-old and two-month-old. She of all people was in the best place to identify with my mom, who also had had two little ones.

Following much contemplation Elizabeth, forever my Betsy Boop, crafted and e-mailed me this insightful message:

> *Hi Moooomer -*
> *I was thinking about when you were born*
> *and how you feel you were such a burden*
> *on your mom and dad.*
>
> *I know without a doubt that the only sad-*
> *ness they had was due to the fact that they*
> *felt you were never going to live a normal*
> *and happy life. Your mom wasn't depressed*
> *that you lived, she was depressed thinking*
> *how hard your life was going to be. They*
> *weren't sad that they got a "crippled" baby,*

they were sad for your future.
As a mom I want nothing but the absolute
best for Bri and Luka. If something was
different with them, I'd be devastated be-
cause I only want them to be happy.

So on your birthday CELEBRATE the fact
that what your mom was so afraid of didn't
happen because you are living the life she
hoped and dreamed for you (but never ex-
pected).

WOW! Elizabeth's words set me, her imprisoned mom, free. Her message ushered in new understanding that boot-ed out hurtful memories. Elizabeth figured it out for me so that when March 4th dawned, I awoke with the words to this song on my lips:

When morning gilds the sky,
My heart awakening cries,
May Jesus Christ be praised.[3]

PRAISE is a special word to me because, come to find out, the name Judy means praise. Mom chose my name early in her pregnancy and had the name Judy written on my birth certificate when praise was nowhere to be found. But our omniscient God, who could see my future, knew all along that He would craft me into a woman of praise. When all was said and done praise could not NOT happen.

Yes, I have been the privileged recipient of *Elohim's* plan for good and not for disaster even when I couldn't see Him. Decades later I've heard myself say, "Precious Lord, You were there all the time, weren't You?" And as I've seen Him, praise has been born – praise heaped upon praise. But hark ye! I am still a work in process, and though progress may seem slow at my end, progress is sure, thanks to my tenacious Creator.

One more story: God used my sister Tina's March 4th, 2012 birthday greeting to me to once and for all silence a lifetime of lies. After reading it, I was finally able to give *Elohim*, the God who makes no mistakes, the standing ovation He deserved.

> *On this most Holy Day, March 4, the day God brought you to our family so many years ago this is the proverb I read:*
>
> *Disaster strikes like a cyclone, whirling the wicked away, but the godly have a lasting foundation. (Proverb 10:25 NLT)*
>
> *You, my sweet sister, have brought our family a living and lasting foundation in the person of Jesus Christ. You met Him in your brokenness then passed Him on to the rest of us in our family.*

It wasn't a cyclone whirling us away but Elohim's plan for us all.

Luv U Forever, Your Sister, Tina

What About You?

Have you met *Elohim*, the Creator God yet? He's eager to be known by you. Can you wrap your head around the fact that He made you exactly like you are for a purpose? He designed each facet of your being – the color of your skin, your height, your IQ, your temperament.

You say you don't like His design. I say, then talk to Him about it. Better yet, let Him talk to you about it. Take your dusty Bible off the shelf or go and buy one. For beginners I'd recommend a modern translation like the *New Living Bible* or *The Message*. Join a Bible study, attend a church, and begin the process of learning to know the One who knows you best because He created you.

Maybe you're well along on your journey with God and you are growing in your relationship with Jesus Christ. Can you praise Him for His marvelous creation called YOU?

Not many of us can wholeheartedly applaud each facet of His design for our lives. Given a chance, the majority of us would change one or one hundred facets of His design. I had my list of changes early on, and yes, long strong legs landed at the top of the list. But come to find out, those missing pieces of my body were the very places where I met God and He was able to meet me. Could it be the same for you? Is it possible that your detestable source of pain might be the very place you make the acquaintance of the Creator Himself?

When we fling open the door to *Elohim*, we can begin to make sense of what doesn't make sense. As we allow Him to grow bigger in our lives, discontentment diminishes, trust in His good plan grows, and one day we wake up and hear ourselves belting out praise to this Creator God who makes no mistakes. *You done good, Lord, especially in the area I was sure was Your greatest mistake.*

3

El Elyon

THE MOST HIGH GOD

*The God Who Gives Height and
Dignity to Our Low Places*

Uppie was my number one favorite word as a child. Born with incomplete legs, plus the fact I didn't own a wheelchair, meant I lived my life on the floor. But "Uppie, Daddy, Uppie" got me off that floor onto a seat high up on my dad's shoulders. His six-foot stature took the sting out of my stunted thirty-four-inch height. Perched high, feeling like I could touch the sky, eliminated my need to crane my neck to look my friends in the eye – now they'd have to strain to see me.

At an early age, I wore Shriners-Hospital-designed metal stilts to make me taller. At age ten I traded the metal for hickory-hewn limbs with bending knees, trim legs and feet that could don a closetful of shoes. Those limbs provided just the height I needed. They'd walk me through the day, but come off at night, so once again I became the Short One.

My everlasting shortness caused me to gravitate to anything and everything tall. My closest friend at age five was not a human but a sapling gingko tree growing outside my second floor bedroom window. Just its being there was a comfort as together we watched the neighborhood kids hav-

Judy standing tall on metal stilts

ing fun. To this day seeing a gingko tree puts a skip in my step, and my family knows – forget a pricey present – a card with a gingko leaf inside will bring Mom a joy that money can't buy.

Being forever short guaranteed I stood out in any crowd, though there was the time my shortness saved the day. After I'd grown up, married, had children and was knee deep in motherhood, daughter Elizabeth came home with an assignment. Her middle school Spanish instructor asked the class to draw a family tree selecting a single word for each family member describing their outstanding characteristic. I panicked. *I'll die if she describes me as crippled. What if she picks the word fat?*

I tensed as she penciled *muy baja* next to my name. "What's that? What's that?" I didn't try to hide my eagerness.

"Very short, Mom. That's you with your legs off!"

From the start, my daughters were quite matter-of-fact about my disability. Maybe they figured all moms took their legs off at night. Thankfully for me there was no stigma attached to their mom being forever short. In fact, I was delighted to be showered with love from the girls' classmates and teachers.

The whole town knew Mrs. Squier loved God, so no

one was surprised when I'd tell stories from my Bible. Soon they learned about my favorite Bible character, who I called Shorty Zaccheus, the guy who didn't let his shortness get him down. One creative dude, he high-tailed it up into a sycamore tree when he heard that Jesus was coming to town. When Jesus spotted him, He, the Most High God, invited Himself to his home for dinner. In an instant, Shorty Zaccheus became Jericho's tallest of the tall. Thanks to his shortness, he had a personal encounter with *El Elyon,* the Most High God (read his story in Luke 19:1-10). As with Zaccheus, I have come to believe that my forever shortness flung open the door for the Most High God.

From down under I'd kept my eyes peeled for *El Elyon* sightings throughout the decades. As a homemaker, I would strain to see Him at the tip tops of our 65-foot-tall Monterey pines as I stood under the kitchen skylight washing dishes. At Disneyland, I bent my neck as far back as it would go to see the top of the ten-foot-tall man on stilts. *Hadn't I walked on stilts too?*

Judy encounters *El Elyon* at Kenya's Giraffe Manor

But my most memorable *El Elyon* sighting occurred outside Nairobi in East Africa at a one-of-a-kind bed and breakfast inn called Giraffe Manor. Where else on earth do two domesti-

21

cated giraffe greet your safari van when you arrive, welcome you, then escort you to the front door? Where else are you awakened by God's tallest creature rattling the shutters on your upstairs bedroom window, begging for alfalfa pellets with its eighteen-inch-long tongue? *El Elyon, El Elyon,* I whispered, You are the Lord, Most High, over all the earth. (Author's paraphrase of Psalm 97:9a NASB)

One last Uppie story. I realize now Uppie was age appropriate for me when I was a child, but it felt embarrassingly awkward for me as a grown woman nearing 60 years of age. But what to do when one is wheelchairbound and the path to the night's lodging consists of rocks and broken cement? Indeed my first mission trip

Judy's piggyback ride in Romania

to Romania ended on a high note with pictures to prove it and the perfect metaphor for what *El Elyon* wants to do for each one of us.

More than anything God wants to secure us piggyback fashion between His strong shoulders and whisk us to the top of each day's mountain. What seems impossible for us is an easy jaunt for Him. *Allow Me,* He says. And He waits to see if we'll accept His offer or if we'll turn Him down and limp along on our own.

Could it be that my favorite word – Uppie – is God's favorite word too? I have a hunch that our Father God longs to hear, "Uppie, Daddy, Uppie," and that He delights in seeing our arms reaching up to Him for help. Somehow I can see Him watching longingly from heaven like I watched from my second story bedroom window as the neighborhood kids had all the fun. Could it be God aches to be invited to join in just like I did?

All along I resented being excluded, but I also detested standing out in the crowd. *Can't I just be like everyone else?* Now that I've been seasoned by life, I have to ask, "What's wrong with being different?" Thanks to my shortness I, like Zaccheus, was spotted by Jesus, and I, like Zaccheus, said YES when the Most High God invited Himself to my house for dinner.

In the last book of the Bible, Jesus' good friend the Apostle John quoted Him as saying, *"Look! I stand at the door and knock. If you hear my voice and open the door, I will come in, and we will share a meal together as friends."* (Revelation 3:20 MSG)

He would love to be welcomed not just into our homes, but into our hearts. He waits, sometimes for a lifetime, for us to invite Him in. Jesus wants to spend time with us as friends do over a lunch date or, nowadays, a latte. But even more than a meal together, He longs to share a lifetime together.

Is that good news, or what? And the best news is He extends His invitation to everyone, not just the world's Shorties.

WHAT ABOUT YOU?

Come to find out shortness is not limited to the physical. Six-foot tall people can feel short emotionally, intellectually or socially. A spouse addicted to drugs or alcohol can bring a family to a screaming halt. Learning disorders can make one day at school feel like a year. Shyness can make recess feel like a torture chamber.

Dysfunction can drive us nuts, but the crazy cycle is worth it if it drives us to our knees. No man or woman stands as tall as when they drop to their knees so their shortness can come face to face with *El Elyon,* the Most High God.

Have you met Him yet? He's standing outside the door of your heart patiently waiting to be invited in. He'd like to join you for a meal. You don't have to make it fancy. Macaroni and cheese will be just fine. It's not the food He's after. He wants you to share your life with Him, every part of it, both the highs and the lows.

4

Jehovah

I AM WHO I AM

My Child: Whatever You Need, I AM

I first heard about the great I AM when I was a child and Dad would talk about the I AMs of Jesus in the Gospel of John. I listened carefully but wasn't sure how I AM and I were supposed to fit together.

Dad said there were seven I AM names, including *I am the Son of God, I am the Way, the Truth and the Life and I am the Good Shepherd.* What was it all about? Come to find out, as Dad was telling me the stories, I was actually making a connection with *I am the Light of the World.*

The Light of the World 4

As a five-year-old latchkey kid waiting at home alone for my family, I'd sit at the foot of the parsonage's long inside staircase looking up at a bigger-than-life picture. Holman Hunt's mid-nineteenth-century painting depicts Jesus knocking on a long-unopened, thistle-covered door seeking a relationship with humanity. In some way that strange picture of Jesus, which I later learned was called *The Light of the World,* kept me company, beginning a relationship that would be decades in the making.

As an adult, I remembered Sunday School lessons about a man named Moses in the Old Testament who met the great I AM in a burning bush. Dumbstruck by an on-fire shrub that was not consumed, he queried, "Who are you?" His visitor identified Himself as *I AM who I AM* (Exodus 3:14), which in Hebrew translates into *YAHWEH,* and in English, *Jehovah.* That was the day Moses stood on holy ground, meeting the God who wanted to be known personally, on a first-name basis.

Jehovah shared His great plans for Moses, plans that could only be actualized as a team. Together they went back to Egypt. *Jehovah* infused Moses with the courage he would need to take down the Pharaoh with ten devastating plagues and to free three million plus people from their bondage.

Looking back over my life I think that *Jehovah* and Dad both knew that Little Judy would need courage for her challenges ahead – lengthy hospitalizations, half a dozen surgeries, learning to walk on artificial limbs, social exclusion. *Jehovah* knew that I, the little girl who stayed short, would need chutzpah to walk out of the front door, to crawl up the ladder at the public pool and plop off the high dive. Yes, I would even need courage from above to look in the full-length mirror. *Jehovah* made a promise to be with me, just like He was with Moses.

Early experiences stay with us and steer our thoughts and actions later in life so that sometimes we do things that surprise even ourselves. It was the winter of 2000, and I was fifty-five years old when I announced to my adult daughters and their father, "I want to get a tattoo."

"A tattoo! What are you thinking?" Their alarmed voices became a quartet.

I tried to convince them it was a great idea by explaining, "Everyone knows I have a lead foot when I drive, so just in case I end up as road kill I want whoever finds me to know to Whom I belong. I need a tattoo that reads *I am His and He is mine*."

As I was building up my nerve to actually get the tattoo, my family took action. My Christmas present that year was a silver ID bracelet containing the seven words now branded on my soul: *I am His and He is mine*.

Placing the bracelet on my wrist, I remembered a ring that Dad had given to each of us kids in his Sunday School class half a century earlier inscribed with *I am His and He is Mine*. I loved that ring and was devastated the summer I lost it in the lake at the crippled children's camp.

What about the tattoo, though? My new bracelet satisfied the longing of my heart so that no tattoo was needed. But then I learned that *Jehovah* is the one with the tattoo. In Isaiah 49:16b (TLB) He says, "I have tattooed you upon my palm." All I could think was, "Lord, You beat me to it!"

Thinking back over the decades, I see that the God with the tattoo has not only been with me, He's gone before me every step of the way. He opened the doors at Shriners Hospital so Broken Judy could get mended; He companioned with me in the wilderness years so I would grow strong thanks to my disability. He buoyed my spirit with His Spirit when I left home to attend a university and then left the university to become a bride, a speech pathologist, and eventually the mother of three little girls.

As *Jehovah* guided, empowered and protected Moses, so *Jehovah* guided, empowered and protected me as my artificial limbs and I carried infants and never fell, Velcroing them to my side so they wouldn't run out in traffic. He's with David and me in our retirement years. Every now and then I have to say, "Mr. Squier, you'd better take off your shoes for both of us; we're on Holy Ground."

Jehovah with Moses, *Jehovah* with Mr. and Mrs. Squier, and *Jehovah* with my mother-in-law, Violet Squier. She and I had never talked about our mutual Friend, but I recognized the great I AM immediately at her memorial service when Psalm 46:10 (NIV) was read and identified as her favorite Bible verse, *Be still and know that I AM God.* To think she knew Him too, especially during her final years. Dementia had stolen her winsome spirit, but thankfully she wasn't alone in the stillness. The great I AM was her companion until He escorted her safely Home.

The truth is that the great I AM is ubiquitous – He's everywhere. But He's easy to miss, especially when He shows up in mundane places where holiness is unexpected. I've sensed His presence as I've watched a three-legged dog romping after a ball or as I've observed a blind person feeling their way along a city street with their white cane. And He was as real to me as if I were seated at a Christmas Eve church service, one December 24th when a one-legged black bird landed on the ledge beside no-legged me as I sat outside Costco. One common bird and I with a single leg between us found ourselves standing on holy ground.

Elizabeth Barrett Browning, one of England's most prominent poets of the Victorian era, knew about holy ground. Being an invalid much of her adult life surely helped her to see it. In four short lines she captured the essence of what the great I AM was telling Moses and what He wants to tell you and me:

> *Earth's crammed with heaven,*
> *And every common bush afire with God;*
> *But only he who sees, takes off his shoes –*
> *The rest sit round it and pluck blackberries.*[5]

WHAT ABOUT YOU?

Have you seen Him? For most of us it takes a while. In fact, my description of how I met Him may seem circuitous. But remember it spanned half a century and was progressive, layer upon layer. First Dad introduced me to the *I AMs* of Jesus. Then I learned about Moses and the burning bush. Next came the jewelry – the lost ring as a child and the ID bracelet as an adult. And finally my mother-in-law's favorite verse held the secret: *Be still and know that I am God.* (Psalm 46:10 NIV)

My progression to faith consisted of a truth here building on a truth there with blessed trials added to help me reach the end of my rope. Finally, I embraced *Jehovah* and allowed Him to embrace me.

What about your progression of faith? Where are you in the process? Is life tough right now? A strained relationship, insufficient funds, failing health, or possibly you just received some bad news. Any of the above, though painful, may be just what you need to up the volume on your spiritual hearing aid in order to hear the too-good-to-be-true offer from heaven: *Whatever you need, I AM.*

The New American Standard (NASB) version of Psalm 46:10 reads: *Cease striving and know that I AM God.* I have to keep asking myself, am I striving or am I knowing/trusting the great *I AM*? We can grit our teeth with the attitude, *we'll make it work,* or we can hand it all over to *Jehovah* and let Him bring order out of the chaos of our lives. Inner turmoil or inner peace, which will it be?

Do you recognize the difference between the two choices? I sure do. How I drive my car, the tone of my voice undergirding my words to my husband, even my strokes as I swim laps tell me instantly who's in charge.

Life often comes to a screaming halt, and I must admit – *caught again* – I recognize that I am striving to do life in my own strength. And you? Caught again? What do we do about it? *Jehovah* to the rescue becomes Jesus to the rescue. Humbly, patiently He waits outside the thistle-covered door where you've hung the sign "Go Away, I'll do it Myself." He waits until we finally recognize again and again throughout the day what He knew all along. *Life is impossible without Him. He's got the key. Actually, He is the key.*

In His presence our self-sufficiency is silenced and all striving can cease. And don't forget to take off those shoes as He turns the impossible circumstances of your life into holy ground.

5

Jehovah Raah

THE LORD MY SHEPHERD

*The Shepherd God Who Cares
for Our Every Need*

I met the Shepherd God as a broken-at-birth lamb. I found out fast that being broken means the rest of the sheep don't know what to do with you so they just leave you out. On the whole, I was spared hurtful remarks or bullying, but I still felt big time rejection. Rejection can translate into self-condemnation and the sorry conclusion: I'm a loser.

When I first read *Jehovah Raah's* name in print I liked it. *He's a cheerleader God,* I decided as I began to listen for His cheers. Raah! Raah! Raah! Certainly it didn't happen over night, but over time His cheers replaced the roar of my internal tapes. *Loser! Loser! Loser!* became *Shepherd, I need You now.*

Max Lucado's children's story, *The Crippled Lamb,* is surely my story. A lamb crippled from birth becomes thankful for his exclusion from the everyday activity of the flock because being left out allowed him to be in the right spot at the right time to meet *Jehovah Raah* born in the stable on Christmas Eve.

Judy and Max Lucado

I remember the year I delivered my personal tribute to *Jehovah Raah* as I leaned over our family's life-sized, straw-filled manger during our church's Christmas program.

My Manger Talk

I found it! The Spirit of Christmas.
I found You, Holy Spirit, Spirit of God.

But of course, the manger, lowly, unpretentious.
God's style. God's Way Up is Down!
Jesus did not consider equality with God, a thing
to be grasped, but emptied Himself –
He made Himself NOTHING!
Lord, let us see our lives through the lens of Your manger.

How well I remember the many mangers over the years.
With Dad a minister, my sister and I
were in the middle of the Christmas pageants.
Like a gaggle of geese our Sunday School classes huddled
at the manger half a century ago.
As a little two year old, I remember straining
to peek at Baby Jesus.

Every year, I watched my class grow taller,
some grew so high they looked down into the manger.
Except for me. I was the short one.
Midget-sized. I never grew.

Everyone in the church knew the
preacher's younger daughter
Judy had been born without legs – a broken baby.
What a shame!
Excuse me!
"What a shame doesn't fit at the manger,
does it, Lord?"
You take the shame of this world and translate it
into Holy Ground – a manger miracle.

A major miracle, it was, Lord,
how You fashioned a short, little
crippled girl into a woman of praise.
You were at work behind the scenes.

Mom tells how she knew she'd name me "Judy"
even before I was born.

So on March 4, 1945,
You, God had Your foot in the door for praise.
Come to find out "Judy" means "Praise."
It didn't come overnight.
The honest truth is my parents'
hearts cracked right down the
middle when my birth defect and I arrived.
Life was crammed full
with countless doctor appointments,
trips to the brace man, eventually trips to the prosthetist –
special education, full weeks but lonely weekends.
In the aloneness, somehow the
family piano and I became friends.
With my good right hand and
my deformed left hand I'd peck
out tunes from Dad's favorite hymnal.

And little by little, like the rising of the sun, Your
Glory shone in my life and through my life.
"Not by might, nor by power, but by Your Spirit."
(Zechariah 4:6 NASB)

Together Lord, You and I learned to walk on seven differ-
ent sets of artificial limbs, attended a Big Ten University,
pledged a sorority, and in June, 1968 received

my MS degree in Speech Pathology the same month
as I received my MRS Degree
and became Mrs. David Squier.
And yet these miracles seemed midget-sized alongside
the births of our three daughters.
My friend Marilee said it best:
"Judy, how great God is.
You were born with no legs and
now you have six good legs."

Yes, Lord, kneeling at Your manger, reality hits.
We've got life backwards, don't we?
Our world seeks the spirit of Christmas in the glitz of
Rockefeller Center in New York City.
Instead the Spirit of Christmas is born
in the cold, dark places in our lives
where pain herds us to the warmth of the manger.

What a relief, to be at the manger.
Is there any possibility our churches
could leave mangers out all year?

I can see it now, lines of people, unchurched mingling with
churched, waiting their turn to be close to the manger.

Wait a minute. Do you hear something?
"Baaa, Baaa . . ." "Raah, Raah . . ."
It's a duet coming from the manger.

"Baaa, Baaa." The sacrificial Lamb of God is here
among us to take away the sins of the world –
my sins, your sins.
"Raah, Raah." Jehovah Raah, the Good Shepherd.
God's Hebrew name Raah
sounds like a cheerleader. "Raah, Raah, Raah."
And that's what You've been trying to tell us, isn't it, Jesus?
The Lord, our God has arrived to live among us.
He is a Mighty Savior. He will give you victory.
He will rejoice over you in great gladness.
He will love you and not accuse you.
What? Is that a joyous choir I hear?
No, it is the Lord Himself,
exulting over you in happy song.
(Zephaniah 3:17-18 TLB)

Our spiritual foundation is built one bale of hay at a time through the truth we're taught, intermingled with our everyday experiences. I know now that my seat of honor atop my father's shoulders paved the way for me to feel comfortable riding atop God's broad shoulders. My woodcarving of a shepherd carrying a lamb atop his shoulders (a must-have memento from our trip to the Holy Land) reminds me constantly of the bond that can happen thanks to human brokenness.

As our Israeli tour bus bounced hither and yon, our guide described the intimate relationship between Palestine shepherds and their sheep. She explained how a loving shepherd might go so far as to break a lamb's leg to ultimately break its independent streak. After setting the limb for healing, the shepherd then carries the rambunctious animal atop his shoulders, slowing him down enough to form a bond of trust and dependency.

That's what happened for me! I thought as the light bulb of understanding went on. My broken body resulted in my willingness to be carried by my earthly father and then by my Heavenly Father. Dad's instant responses to my bleating, "Uppie, Daddy, Uppie," led me to believe that *Jehovah Raah's* ears were tuned to my cry.

My cries for help were at their loudest as I entered the uncharted territory of motherhood without legs. "Shepherd, I need You now" became my daily, hourly SOS call. I remember asking the discharge nurse if I could leave my first born at the hospital until the bundle in my nervous arms turned eighteen. The nurse laughed, thinking I was kidding. I wasn't.

How was Legless Judy ever going to manage caring for first one, then another, and yet another helpless bundle at home? Hourly I had to ask myself, "Do I do this task with my legs on or my legs off?" I figured it out one step at a time and thanked the Good Lord for His moment-by-moment help from heaven above. Each night I would stand my artificial limbs in the nursery room closet, park my wheelchair at the foot of the stairway, crawl up the steps to our second story master bedroom, then collapse into bed believing some battle-weary guardian angels were thankful for yet another day being over.

Everyone knew that David's real job began at 5:00 p.m. when he arrived home from work. And yes, the girls had to pitch in as soon as they could toddle. "You help me and I help you" kept the Squier family afloat. But deep down inside I felt totally inadequate. I was relieved no one watched the unorthodox ways I did things.

I shouted, "Amen!" when someone gave me Robert Kemper's book *An Elephant's Ballet: The*

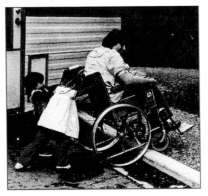
Daughters Elizabeth and Emily assisting Mom

Story of One Man's Successful Struggle with Sudden Blindness. This pastor's frustration resonated with my own, and I would catch myself singing his tune, "It may not be a good ballet, but it's amazing that I do it at all."[6]

Watching other moms effortlessly do life with a baby on their hip, seeing these fleet of foot women on the slide with their toddlers (when my wheelchair and I couldn't traverse the tan bark), just watching their strong legs jump in and out of their Suburbans, I'd think to myself, *I'm a loser! Loser! Loser!*

The good news is that *Jehovah Raah* doesn't just see our pain; He feels it, and in my case He did something about it. Raah! Raah! Raah! One summer day, I received a phone call from the Family Research Council in Washington D.C. A woman named Sarah called to tell me their annual Anschutz banquet was being planned; this year's honorees would be three disabled Americans and guess what? I was one of them. So in November 1991 the five Squiers were flown to our nation's capital where we received the red carpet treatment, culminating in the banquet. Awards were presented, including a fifteen pound bronze statue, identical to the one

Judy admiring Jehovah Raah at Vintage Faith Church in Santa Cruz, CA

housed in the Smithsonian Museum. The engraving at the base of a mother eagle feeding her three eaglets still brings goose bumps of amazement to my soul: *The Marian Pfister Anschutz Award Presented to Judy Squier in Recognition of Her Dedication to Protecting, Encouraging and Strengthening the American Family.*

Raah! Raah! Raah! Above the applause in the Mayflower hotel's banquet hall, I could hear the cheers from heaven.

My Heavenly Father and my earthly father (who had gone to heaven two years earlier) were well pleased with this crippled little lamb. Yes, I had learned to walk on seven different sets of artificial limbs, but best of all, I'd grown strong spiritual limbs in the process – spiritual limbs which my friend Mary says *run people right into the Good Shepherd's presence.*

That was the year God promoted me from His shoulders to the dance floor. No longer an elephant ballerina, my favorite waltz partner became and forever will be *Jehovah Raah! Raah! Raah!*

WHAT ABOUT YOU?

Do you feel like an elephant ballerina? Clumsy, having two left feet, bulky, inept, slow, out to lunch? Step one in learning to waltz involves jumping up on *Jehovah Raah's* broad shoulders; in that spot it's guaranteed you'll allow Him to take the lead.

Now, while you're up there, lean forward and listen to what He has to say to you: *I love you, little lamb. You are my heart's delight. Forget about your weakness. Actually what you see as a weakness, in My eyes is a strength. Thanks to it, you allowed Me to rescue you, right? That's what a Shepherd's for, you know. Throw away the old tapes of condemnation. Loser is not in heaven's vocabulary. Listen for my words of affirmation. I'm your Cheerleader, remember? Raah! Raah! Raah!*

6

Jehovah Shammah

THE LORD IS THERE

No Matter Where You Are,
I Am with You

I was sixty years old when I sought the services of a Christian counselor to help me figure out some of the contradictions simmering inside of me. Every Thursday morning for three years I'd park my wheelchair at the foot of a small stairway and crawl up the six steps to her office for my hour-long appointment. As I talked she would listen, always affirming my value. Little Judy and Adult Judy had themselves a cheerleader, as my counselor companioned with me down Memory Lane.

One day she asked me to describe my loneliness as a little girl. After a few minutes I described midget-sized me, maybe I was eight years old, sitting on the curb under a catalpa tree, pretend-smoking one of its long cigar-like pods. I sat purposelessly watching the cars go by, realizing that with no friends and an empty calendar, life was passing me by.

She asked, "Were you sitting there alone, Little Judy?"

I had to think for a minute. Finally I answered, "Oh my, I wasn't alone. Jesus was sitting beside me."

"Did you talk to each other?" she asked.

Hmmm. Did we talk? I strained to remember and finally reported, "I told Him I was hungry and said, 'Let's go to the corner store and get some ice cream.'"

No deep spiritual relationship at that point. In fact, in that pit of aloneness, I don't recall sensing Jesus present with me. But hindsight assured me He'd been there all along, when I finally saw His presence as an adult, if only in the rear-view mirror.

> *Christ with me, Christ before me,*
> *Christ behind me, Christ in me,*
> *Christ beneath me, Christ above me,*
> *Christ on my right, Christ on my left,*
> *Christ when I lie down, Christ when I sit,*
> *Christ when I stand,*
> *Christ in the heart of everyone who thinks of me,*
> *Christ in the mouth of everyone who speaks of me,*
> *Christ in every eye that sees me,*
> *Christ in every ear that hears me.*
> *Amen[7]*

Fast-forward to my college years. The above prayer of St Patrick buoyed my fledgling faith as I, with a brand new understanding of a God Who is There, returned to the University of Illinois for my junior year. I needed His courage because, after my two years of life as a casual student, the year of reckoning had come. Would I sink or swim? God doesn't want us to sink so He arranged for the spiritual boost I would need to swim.

One month before returning to school while visiting Uncle Walt and Aunt Ginny, I told Aunt Ginny about my fears of flunking out of the university. She explained to me that God could help me, and that He cared about every detail of my life. She continued, "Judy, God wants to have a personal relationship with you. Jesus died on the cross, not only to save you eternally, but to save you daily as you depend on Him. He waits outside the locked door of your life until you invite Him in."

Did I want to do that? *You mean I can know God on a personal basis? You mean He can actually intervene in circumstances and save me from failure?*

Her answer was affirmative. And so was mine.

August 14, 1965 went down in history as my spiritual birthday – the day I prayed a simple prayer and opened the thistle-covered door of my life to Jesus. "*Behold, I stand at the door and knock,*" He says, "*if anyone hears My voice and opens the door, I will come in to him and will dine with him, and he with Me.*" (Revelation 3:20 NASB) By faith I knew Jesus entered my life, so I cleared a spot for Him at mealtime in the Allen Hall cafeteria at the University of Illinois, then the next year in the classy dining room at the Alpha Gamma Delta house.

Only He could have led me to the one sorority on campus with half a dozen Christian sorority sisters who preferred Friday night Campus Crusade for Christ meetings over weekend drinking parties. Not only did He lead me, He was with me, transforming me from a near-flunk-out to a serious student with a five-point average.

Sunday Sweet Sunday became my favorite day of the week, the day I got to go to God's House. As a new person in Christ, I drew strength from every word of the sermon and comfort as the organ played familiar hymns from my childhood. My lips quivered when the service ended. *Goodbye God. The week ahead looks frightful, but I'll see you next week!* It was a while before I realized, *Jehovah Shammah* can never be left behind.

Aunt Ginny sent me weekly letters containing Bible promises to encourage me. When I wrote to her about my doubts – *what if this new Friend leaves me?* – she wrote back to say doubts were normal, especially doubts about eternal security in Christ. She sent me a Bible promise from Hebrews which I clung to for dear life: *for He (God) Himself has said, I will not in any way fail you nor give you up nor leave you without support. (I will) not, (I will) not, (I will) not in any degree leave you helpless, nor forsake nor let (you) down, (relax My hold on you!). Assuredly not!* (Hebrews 13:5b AMP)

Over time I finally understood! He was with me in class and out of class. He was with me during dreaded final exams. He was with me in June 1968 when Miss Rieder became Mrs. Squier. He swung open the door for my first job as a speech pathologist at the renowned Stanford Hospital Medical Center supplying the strength and wisdom I needed as I struggled with a new career.

He led; I followed the stepping stones, from admitting I needed a Savior, to praying the prayer of salvation, to the Sunday I realized I couldn't leave the Omnipresent One behind even if I wanted to. As a wife, as a career woman, I met with Him regularly in the mornings before work – studying the Bible, talking and listening to Him in prayer, journaling to process life's conundrums, reading Christian books.

I learned about Brother Lawrence, a 17th century monk, who blessed others as he practiced *Jehovah Shammah's* presence in a mundane kitchen, cooking meals and scrubbing pots.[8] I took God's presence to heart. Maybe I went a little overboard the day I met a speech pathology colleague for lunch at Pizza Hut. Guarding the empty chair at our table, making sure no one took it, I could see my friend was perplexed. "It's for Jesus," I whispered.

The more I found Him present for me, the more I wanted to hear about other people's God sightings. My cousin Carol sensed Him near as she faced a lifelong fear of the moment of death. Undergoing extensive jaw work, she panicked during the administration of anesthesia. In her panic her doctor touched her hand, repeating over and over, "Carol, I am here." God's deep peace came over her as the doctor's words translated into Jesus saying, "Carol, I am here." Sensing *Jehovah Shammah's* presence eliminated any present or future fear of the moment of death.

Sir Ernest Shackleton tells of his experience at the tragic end of the Imperial Trans-Antarctic Expedition in 1916.

With his ship *Endurance* ice bound, he and two crew members fought to survive, enduring a thirty-six-hour journey on foot across treacherous glaciers. Exhausted, willing their feet to keep moving, each of them concluded, "It seemed we were four not three."[9] Scientists call it the Third Man Factor - how those in dire peril have felt a sudden presence. I call it The Lord is There, *Jehovah Shammah.*

Shackleton's story reminds me of Shadrach, Meshach and Abednego in the Old Testament, the three captive Hebrew lads who were thrown into a fiery furnace in Babylon. When King Nebuchadnezzar looked in the furnace door, he exclaimed, "*Look! I see four men loosed and walking about in the midst of the fire without harm, and the appearance of the fourth is like a son of the gods!*" (Daniel 3:25 NASB)

Author Sarah Young, longing to experience God's presence, tells how early on she'd approach her quiet times with pen in hand, ready to hear and record Jesus' thoughts. Her times of meditation changed from her talking to God into a dialogue *with* God, as His thoughts came to her mind. Her popular devotional, *Jesus Calling*, which I love, is written in the first-person singular, containing Jesus' words to us all.[10]

My dear friend Phyllis, just a week after losing her husband of almost 59 years, announced one day with a big smile, "Jesus talks to me every morning, when I read my *Jesus Calling* devotional."

WHAT ABOUT YOU?

But as for me, I get as close to Him as I can! I have chosen him and I will tell everyone about the wonderful ways he rescues me. (Psalm 73:28 TLB)

Are you moving as close to Him as you can get? Or are you moving in the opposite direction? Like an anchorless ship adrift at sea, we can move away from Him without even noticing.

Whether we acknowledge it or not, God is omnipresent. We can't go anywhere that He isn't. And yet God gives us free will so it is possible to do life with or without Him. *If God feels far away, guess who moved?* We get busy. We forget about God. We get stressed. Life becomes more and more complicated, and finally, troubles bring us to a screaming halt.

Jesus said in the Beatitudes, *"You're blessed when you're at the end of your rope. With less of you there is more room for God and his rule."* (Matthew 5:3 MSG) I reached the end of my rope in college and finally understood that the God of the universe wanted to become my personal Savior, my Boss, and my Best Friend. Finally I heard Jesus knocking on the door of my life; finally I understood He wanted a relationship with me and that He wanted more than anything to save me from my self-destructive course. How could He do that? He won the battle on an old rugged cross. My part would be to admit my need, to receive Him and allow Him to become my Boss and my BFF – Best Friend Forever.

Have you reached the end of your rope, dear reader? Maybe once upon a time you prayed and asked Jesus into your life but are now adrift at sea. Or maybe you are currently in relationship with God, but feel alone and defeated.

Jehovah Shammah revealed Himself to His people at a very low point in Jewish history described in the book of Ezekiel. The prophet and God's people were now captives in Babylon. Back home their Holy City, Jerusalem, had been destroyed with their temple ransacked. When their beloved city was no more, *Jehovah Shammah* visited the prophet Ezekiel with the following message of hope: *...The name of the city from that day shall be, 'The Lord is There.'* (Ezekiel 48:35 NASB)

When we lose our greatest love, God is there to meet us in life's ruins. When it can't get worse, God shows up with the same message of hope 2500 years later: *No matter how bad your life is right now, I'm with you. I promise to bring you through. Are you willing to let Me?*

7

El Roi

THE GOD WHO SEES

*The God Who Companions
with Us in Our Pain*

In my heart I imagined myself the poster child for the neighborhood outcast in Berwyn, Illinois in the 1950s. Everyone knew which house on the block was the home of the midget-sized girl who walked (and ran) on metal stilts. Add buckteeth and, it's true, it was not a pretty picture. Haley Elementary School, just three blocks away, refused my admission. Why? They said I was an insurance risk.

With no adaptive sports in those days I was relegated to the role of full time spectator *until* the neighborhood gang discovered this girl could turn a jump rope. Who wouldn't die for the privilege of being the permanent rope turner while kids from far and near jumped to their hearts' content? It killed me. Just like summer mornings killed me when someone from down the street stood on our front porch yelling for their best friend to come out and play. I awoke to the cold reality – they were crooning my sister Tina's name, never mine.

Extreme loneliness marked my childhood and 'tween

years, but bad only got worse when I was a teenager. I lived life vicariously through Tina's full social calendar. Hourly I drooled over her tantalizingly sweet, popular life. I watched her friends come, and I watched my sis and her friends go. Then my unevent-filled life began in the company of solitude and boredom.

Hagar and the Angel in the Desert [11]

O happy day – the day I discovered that God sees and companions with the outcasts. The Old Testament records the story of Hagar, a run away Egyptian slave girl, not even a follower of *Jehovah*, who received a personal visit from God Himself. *El Roi,* the God Who Sees, saw Hagar's pain, talked to her, encouraged her and instructed her. (Learn more about Hagar in Genesis 16 and 21.)

God gives us Bible characters with stories that resonate with our own stories. My friend Zaccheus was a shorty just like me, and wasn't Hagar's rejection just like mine? Unlike Hagar I had a family that loved me and supported my every need, but as much as they wanted to, they couldn't control actions and reactions outside our front door. Mom and Dad hurt along with me but never verbalized the emotional pain of raising me, their wilting wallflower, under the same roof as my social butterfly sister.

More than half a century has passed since Little Judy was the outcast and since my family struggled for my inclusion. Still today society struggles with what to do with individuals who don't fit into the established programs. Granted, there's been much progress since the '50s – advances in technology, educational mainstreaming, adaptive sports, accessible public buildings and public transportation; but there are still oversights in the world of disability. *Didn't I just crawl up the steps onto the transport bus from the airport to the rent-a-car lot because there was no lift? El Roi* sees it all and companions with each one of us, giving this 68-year-old lady with no legs the strength to climb those steps and hoist up into the seat.

And I rejoice that *El Roi,* the God Who Sees, has provided a place that many marginalized families call heaven on earth – Joni and Friends Family Retreats (www.joniand-friends.org). Joni Eareckson Tada sustained a broken neck as a 17-year old following a dive into shallow water in Chesapeake Bay. She traded her social popularity as she learned firsthand how it feels to be cast out of life's normals. Quadriplegia stole her physical prowess and her independence, shattering her plans and dreams for the future. As Joni experienced life's losses and exclusion, Joni and Friends (JAF) became God's perfect pick to create retreats for families affected by disability.

At JAF Family Retreats all over the world, physical and spiritual rest, relaxation and rejuvenation replace a family's

Joni and Judy   Joni's wheelchair drawing[12]

battleground called daily life. A newfound dignity boots the label "damaged goods" out the door as short-term missionaries, retreat staff, families and individuals affected by disability meet *El Roi* – the God who comes alongside outcasts, eyeball to eyeball.

One little camper with cerebral palsy hit the nail on the head when he said, "I love Joni Camp because I have fun instead of being made fun of." Moms and dads, suddenly escorted out of isolation and welcomed into deep relationships, have been heard to say, "You too? I thought we were the only ones." And after five days of watching God's fun-loving, gifted folks with Down syndrome, you can't help but wonder why Down syndrome wasn't called Up syndrome.

I celebrate the emotional and spiritual strengthening of individuals and families thanks to programs like the JAF Family Retreats. But there are still those who, in their human suffering, seemingly fall through the cracks. A friend named Patrick speaks of his years of physical and emotional abuse as a child from the hand of an out-of-control father. Year after year Patrick would plead, *Help, I need help. Is there a God up there? Please help me!*

Heaven's unending silence added insult to Patrick's injury. Then came the day when, as a bitter teenager alone on a beach, Patrick's emotional Mt. Vesuvius erupted, and he raged at God. *Where were You when I needed You? Where were you?*

Heaven's silence broke when *El Roi,* the God who is there for the underdog answered him. *Remember the night your Dad's eye conveyed this is the night I'm going to kill you? You're alive aren't you?*

Patrick's heart melted, as he finally understood that the God who sees all, had in fact seen it all. Patrick knows now that no suffering is wasted. God used the pain to equip him to become a much sought after pastor/counselor with an extraordinary ability to empathize with human suffering because he's been there. And the God Who Sees was there with him all along just as He is with you and me.

WHAT ABOUT YOU?

Do you or a loved one take the prize for being the shunned or shamed poster child in the family or on the block? Are you the target of someone's undeserved wrath? Or maybe your hell on earth is your own making. Maybe your bad choices have destroyed your family or ruined yours or someone else's reputation. Has your self-respect been dealt a deathblow by your hand or another's?

You are not alone. Individuals who were lonely, friendless, and discarded by society are all over the pages of the Bible. King David's family of origin didn't even remember to bring the shepherd boy in when the prophet Samuel was looking for the future king. Hannah's noisy grief over her barrenness was misinterpreted by the priest to be drunkenness. And Jesus, the King of Kings, was born to a peasant couple in a stinky stable because there was no room in the inn.

Shunned by the world but seen and visited by God. That's been my story. Is it yours also? God wants you to know that you have never been alone – knocked down maybe, but never abandoned. As you get your bearings, as your eyes focus, behold another Traveler with battle scars from a battle won long ago.

We despised him and rejected him —
a man of sorrows, acquainted with bitterest grief.
We turned our backs on him and

looked the other way when he went by.
He was despised and we didn't care.
Yet it was our grief he bore,
our sorrows that weighed him down.
And we thought his troubles were a punishment from God,
for his own sins!
But he was wounded and bruised for our sins.
He was chastised that we might have peace;
He was lashed – and we were healed.
(Isaiah 53:3-5 TLB)

Pulling yourself up by your bootstraps is not in the Bible. Being one's own savior is not in the Bible either. The wounds of Jesus Christ were received on our behalf. His wounds can heal ours if we let them. Are you ready to lean into *El Roi's* embrace and welcome Him as your Savior? Together you and He can survive any and all impossible situations. In Him you can find peace though all hell is raging around you. And He promises you will rise just like He did.

8

Jehovah Nissi

THE LORD IS MY BANNER

The God Who Crowns Us a Winner

I love the word independent. That's what I wanted to be when I grew up. Independent. Needing no help from anyone. I'd had more than my share of helpers. My name was Short One because I needed to ride atop a Tall One's shoulders. With no wheelchair, I rode in a stroller. No way can a stroller be self-propelled so Ms. Independence had to wait for a push. *Grrrr.* And to this day I ache when I remember sitting on the couch watching Mom and Dad perspire and groan lugging this college coed's wardrobe down the stairs and out to the car. Shame pinned me to the mat as I watched and they worked.

Moses of the Old Testament was stripped of his independence, but instead of feeling shame, he built an altar to *Jehovah Nissi,* acknowledging God as his banner. Moses needed super-human strength the day God assigned him to the hillside to hold the shepherd's staff heavenward so the agrarian Israelites could defeat the highly qualified army of Amalek. Joshua was on the front lines while Moses held up the same staff that God used to deliver His people out of

Egypt, the same staff that had parted the Red Sea. Because Moses' arms were fatiguing and because Joshua's motley army only rallied when Moses' arms were up, God provided two helpers to get the job done. Aaron and Hur sat tired Moses down on a rock and held his hands high until sunset. The battle was won and to commemorate the victory Moses built an altar calling it *Jehovah Nissi —The Lord is My Banner.* (Exodus 17:8-18)

But there's more tucked into the story. Amalek, the enemy army, is a picture in Scripture of the flesh that opposes the things of God. Historically, Amalek was the grandson of Esau, the twin brother who valued his fleshly cravings more than the spiritual as he traded his birth right for a bowl of porridge. The Amalekites were self-reliant and confident of their slam-dunk victory. The Israelites needed and relied on the strength of the Lord knowing that their shepherd army was outnumbered big time.

Who needs God's help when victory is a slam-dunk? Strength brings self-reliance and self-reliance brings independence. Independence from God, doing it my way, has my vote for the best definition of sin.

The Amalek of the Old Testament... I know him well. And I know that my fleshly desire for self-sufficiency wars daily with God's plan that He be my sufficiency. Paul clarifies the issue in Philippians 4:13: *I have strength for all things in Christ Who empowers me [I am ready for anything and equal to anything through Him Who infuses inner strength into me; I am self-sufficient in Christ's sufficiency].* (AMP)

Come to find out God does not glory in our strength but in our weakness, because *when I am weak then I am strong.* (II Corinthians 12:10 NASB) God, who designed us for relationship, intends for our weaknesses not to shame us, but to herd us to the Shepherd, to help make our independence dependent and to build intimacy with Him.

Our answer *yes* to His offer of help from above also builds community as we become willing to receive help from below. Reliance on God and reliance on the Aaron-and-Hur-helpers He provides, equip us to win life's battles. But both require a willingness to receive help. The hitch comes when our flesh takes pride in all-sufficiency, refusing help from an outside source. We carry on as if *God helps those who help themselves* is a Bible verse even when we know it isn't.

Being willing to receive help is still one of my battle-fields. When I hear, "May I help you put your wheelchair in the car?" Ms. Independence replies, "No thanks, I'll save your offer until I really need it." Invariably when I need help and there's none to be had, I get mad. What a vicious cycle. A gentleman friend recently voiced a new perspective. "Judy, do you realize you are denying us the blessing when you refuse our help?"

I realize now how independence was reinforced during decades of physical therapy. No therapist ever volunteered to pick me up when I fell down on my artificial limbs; they coached me how to get thyself up and to stand on thine own two feet. Add to that humanity's instinctive pride in being self-sufficient, and the stage is set for a battle between self-reliance and God-reliance.

I admitted my zealous self-sufficiency at a women's retreat recently. Feeling convicted by the keynote speaker's messages on the necessity of our flesh yielding to God's Spirit in us, I concluded, *I'm at a 50/50. My flesh wins half of the time; God's Spirit in me gets the other half.* My admission of the embarrassing truth resulted in dead silence from the other women in the small group I was facilitating. *Now I know I am the World's Worst Christian.* The Shamer let me have it.

Some people lick their wounds in the closet. Not I. Noticing the retreat speaker in front of me the next day in the breakfast line, I sheepishly confessed, "You've been teaching about the importance of the spirit winning in its battle with the flesh, and I'm embarrassed to admit it, but I think I'm a 50/50 – 50% of the time God's Spirit in me wins, but 50% of the time my flesh wins." She spun on her heels not hiding her amazement. "You mean you're that good?"

I shocked her in the breakfast line, and she returned the shock wave in her final talk when she shared her secret for victory over Amalek. "It works every time," she confided. "The sure way to conquer your strong will is to lose." Lose? That's the last thing any of us would choose. She supported her conclusion. Jesus shared His secret before going to the cross: *If you cling to your life, you will lose it; but if you give up your life for me, you will find it.* (Matthew 10:39 NLT)

God's Spirit in me gets it, but my flesh digs in the heels of my artificial limbs and goes *GRRRRR!* Fortunately God provides role models with skin on – fellow cross-followers who have relinquished their wills to the Lord, even when it nearly killed them.

I can still hear Kim Neher's love song to God twenty years after her heartbreaking ordeal. Her family's battlefield was cancer. Their five-year-old son Ryan was the warrior, battling for his life. As his health declined, his family and friends all over the world prayed for God's miracle. The battle was lost. Or was it? The banner of *Jehovah Nissi* was flying high the morning of Ryan's memorial service, when his mom awoke with a praise song on her lips: *I love you, Lord. I worship You. May my song of praise bring You joy.* Her will had surrendered. In losing, even losing a son, she won as her soul waved *Jehovah Nissi's* victory banner.

My friend Rick Copus sings victory songs while riding his bike hundreds of miles a week. Not just an ordinary bike, mind you, but a 7-speed bicycle with a wheelchair attached to the front. Seated in the wheelchair is his adult daughter Autumn, who has cerebral palsy and a bipolar condition. As Autumn's mood disorder became increasingly agitating over the years, the family discovered that movement calmed her. Rick's feet grew weary pushing her wheelchair around the house, then around the block. Then finally came the bike idea.

Rick, a professional singer, has a favorite song he wails as he and his daughter take to the bike paths in Bakersfield, California. *The name of the Lord is a strong tower, the righteous runs into it and is safe.* (Proverbs 18:10 NASB) I can see the victory banner of Rick's *Jehovah Nissi* waving in the breeze as he and contented Autumn whiz by. Rick practices what he sings as he pedals his way into the protection of God's name.

Jehovah Nissi's banner stands tallest on our altars of sacrifice – when we finally give up our will, even when it means losing. Our flesh can finally dwell secure when we release our grip and invite the Lord to have His way in us. The battle is not for sissies but we become valiant warriors as we surrender to *Jehovah Nissi's* orchestration of His victory team.

> *Onward Christian soldiers, marching as to war.*
> *With the cross of Jesus going on before;*
> *Christ, the royal Master, leads against the foe;*
> *Forward into battle, see His banners go.*[13]

WHAT ABOUT YOU?

Are you willing to lose your life? Our flesh is like an untamed, ravenous lion. Afraid of danger, we become dangerous. Afraid of failure, we devour anyone who gets in our way. Afraid of being left out, we push our way to the center or pout in a corner. Afraid our appetites will go unmet, we engorge ourselves with food or drink or indulge in other sources of gratification. *Lose my life? Are you kidding?*

But Jesus-in-us sets His face like flint and invites us to march with Him to the cross. Carrying His cross forces us to be God-reliant. *God, You are our only hope. I can't do this without You.*

I remember how hard I clung to Him as a mom-without-limbs caring for three little ones. Holding high *Jehovah Nissi's* banner (at times with sweaty palms and quaking artificial knees) I would review my battle cry: *Anyone who wants to follow Me must put aside his own desires and conveniences and carry his cross with him everyday and keep close to Me.* (Luke 9:23 TLB) His words kept me close to Him. Keeping close to Him made all the difference in the world. It did for me and it can for you.

9

Jehovah Tsidkenu

THE LORD OUR RIGHTEOUSNESS

The God Who Can Right All Our Wrongs

I remember wondering about heaven as a little girl and assuring myself, *surely being crippled will guarantee me a spot.* I learned otherwise attending a Billy Graham Evangelistic Crusade in the summer of 1955. Walking cautiously on my brand new, first set of artificial limbs, I and thousands of others of all ages entered New York City's Madison Square Garden. Awkwardly, I climbed the stairway to an empty row of seats high up in the massive arena.

Even at the young age of ten, my attention was glued to Billy Graham's sermon about a personal relationship with Jesus. I was drawn in by the closing hymn, "Just as I Am," and wanted to go forward for the altar call but couldn't manage the steep stairway without help. I didn't see it then but I see it now in my soul's rear view mirror. Jesus climbed the stairs to meet me right there in my seat. *No stairway, not even the Grand Canyon, could keep Him from a heart that is opening its door to Him.*

My encounter that day was but a stepping stone toward God. I had mountains ahead, mastering those legs, surviving the years of exclusion, coming to believe that I was loved and loveable. Somehow I lost Jesus in the shuffle. For the time being, I would be content being known *as the brave girl who walked on artificial limbs.* My life mission at that point was to be an inspiration, and I even had a favorite hymn to clinch it.

Make Me a Blessing

Verse 1:
Out on the highways and byways of life
Many are weary and sad, carry the sunshine
where darkness is rife – making the sorrowing glad.

Chorus:
Make me a blessing, make me a blessing
Out of my life may Jesus shine
Make me a blessing O Savior I pray
Make me a blessing to someone today.

Verse 2:
Tell the sweet story of Christ and his Love
Tell of His power to forgive
Others will trust Him if only prove
True every moment you live.[14]

Even as a college coed, I wanted to be a blessing and no more. No way did I want to go overboard with the Jesus stuff. When a campus missionary accused me of practicing

"Christianity minus Christ," I supported my stand with the first stanza of *Make Me a Blessing*. Surprisingly, she knew the song too and challenged me with stanza two and the chorus. Hearing the words nailed me.

Slowly but surely I came to understand that it's impossible to do Christianity without Christ. I finally got it. Jesus was the one and only One who could live the Christian life, and He was the sole ticket to eternal life. By faith I accepted *Jehovah Tsidkenu* as my own righteousness and plugged my name into John 3:16.

For God so loved Judy,
that He gave His only begotten Son,
so that Judy, who now believes in Him,
shall not perish, but have eternal life.
(Author's paraphrase, NASB)

Finally I understood that my spot in heaven was guaranteed, not because of my disability, but because of what God's only begotten Son accomplished on my behalf.

Chinese symbol: *I under the Lamb am righteous*

The saving work of *Jehovah Tsidkenu* is memorialized by Ruth Bell Graham at the Billy Graham Library in Charlotte, North Carolina. Her tombstone contains a Chinese character that means *I Under the Lamb Am Righteous*. The top of the symbol means *lamb* and the bottom means *me, myself and I.* The Lamb is the Son of God who died on the cross in our place. His blood poured out for mankind is humanity's only source of righteousness. His gift is free of charge to all who believe and who will position themselves under His authority.

Come to find out, righteousness in Christ BEGINS with a recognition of one's own unrighteousness. Humanity needs to see its need of a Savior. The Bible teaches that *all have sinned and fall short of the glory of God.* (Romans 3:23 NASB) *All* includes me and *all* includes you, no matter how good we are.

The prophet Jeremiah teaches that *the human heart is the most deceitful of all things, and desperately wicked. Who really knows how bad it is?* (Jeremiah 17:9 NLT) My doctor friend, Marilee, enlightened me one day when she said, "Judy, the human heart is so slippery, that no surgeon can pick it up."

That's the hard-to-swallow bad news, but the good news is that righteousness becomes ours the moment we put our faith in Jesus Christ. From then on God the Father sees us wrapped in His Son's robe of righteousness. Fully dressed, fully forgiven, we then experience God's great work of conforming us to the image of His Son. We become His work in progress bearing the title *Under Construction.*

I've always delighted in Ruth Bell Graham's playful, yet Rock solid style even until the end. I expect hers is the only epitaph that reads, "End of construction. Thank you for your patience." While touring Billy Graham's Conference Center,

The Cove, we learned through the Grahams' daughter, Gigi, that her mother chose those words years before her death after seeing them on a road construction sign. Mrs. Graham's comment to her family was, "What a marvelous image for the Christian life – a work under construction until we go to be with God. That's what I want as my epitaph."

Saint Bernards to the Rescue[15]

I expect millions of sermons have been preached through the centuries and around the world on The Lord Our Righteousness. My favorite is actually a children's story called "Barry the St. Bernard" about a rescue dog high up in the Alps. His job, as well as his joy, was to search out lost travelers in severe winter storms. He was trained to find them, warm them with his big furry body, and lick them with his warm tongue so that they would revive. Ultimately his purpose was to lead them to safety.

He did his job perfectly and passionately until one day the delirious traveler he came to save mistook him for a wolf and stabbed him repeatedly with his hunting knife. Bleeding and fatally wounded, Barry crawled inch-by-inch back to the alpine hospice leaving a trail of blood, a lifeline for the saved traveler.[16]

I can't help but think, *that's exactly what Jesus our Savior did for us.* He saw our helpless and hopeless state. He searched us out. He took on Himself our fatal deathblows and His blood left the trail for us to follow Him Home.

For me, Romans 5:10-11 says it all: *If, when we were at our worst, we were put on friendly terms with God by the sacrificial death of his Son, now that we're at our best, just think of how our lives will expand and deepen by means of his resurrection life! Now that we have actually received this amazing friendship with God, we are no longer content to simply say it in plodding prose. We sing and shout our praises to God through Jesus, the Messiah!* (MSG)

WHAT ABOUT YOU?

Are you ready to begin an amazing friendship with the God of the Universe? Pride will tell you, *I don't need Him.* Self-sufficiency will tell you, *I'm doing great without Him.* False humility will tell you, *He's got much bigger things to worry about than me!*

I say you are wrong on all three counts. Indeed you do need Him; you actually aren't doing great. And to convince you of your value, I add – if you were the only one on earth, Jesus would have died so He could save you.

Jesus' gift of righteousness is free.
Jesus' gift of righteousness will set you free.
He's standing outside the thistle-covered door
of your heart waiting for you to open it.
He's waiting to be invited in.
He's waiting to give you the purpose you lack.
He's waiting to champion you through circumstances
that are humanly impossible.
He's waiting to convince you that you are loved
and that you are loveable.
He's waiting to make what's wrong in your life right.

Hopefully you are asking, "How do I sign up?" Putting your name in John 3:16 is a stepping stone toward making *Jehovah Tsidkenu's* Righteousness your righteousness.

For God so loved _____,
that He gave His only begotten Son,
so that _____ who now believes in Him
shall not perish, but have eternal life.

Date:_____

10

El Shaddai

THE ALL-SUFFICIENT GOD
The God Whose Supply Exceeds Life's Demands

I remember Dad entreating the aid of God Almighty by voicing His name in a crisis, just like Father Abraham did in the Old Testament. But I didn't entreat God Almighty myself until I experienced my own moment of truth in my middle years. For two decades of marriage I had depended on David's long, strong legs like they were my own – especially when we became parents. David's legs were Judy's legs until his fateful fall in 1990. The compound fracture of his ankle, subsequent hospitalization, three surgeries and long recovery, meant my artificial limbs and I were on our own.

Too battle weary to pretend, my blunt honesty jumped out one Sunday at our church's coffee table. The lady's question was innocent enough. "Judy, how's the family?" My intense response caused both of us to spill our hot drinks. "I'm dying. I don't think I'm going to make it. Motherhood is killing me!"

That was the Sunday I learned the week's truth-to-live-by *after* the sermon: an honest answer may be unwelcome when one asks *how are you?* My friend's verbal spanking

Judy with daughters in stair step formation

let me know in no uncertain terms that being overwhelmed was not politically-correct. "Motherhood is difficult for everyone, Judy! You are no special case."

No sympathy indeed from that sister in the faith, but *El Shaddai* heard my distress call. He let me know that human inadequacy does not warrant guilt or shame; in fact, our inadequacy can become a blessing when it unplugs our ears so we can hear His invitation – *If you will give Me all of your inadequacies, and come to Me in believing faith, I will give you all that I have.*

Instantly, thanks to my need, *El Shaddai,* the All-Sufficient God took up residence at the Squier home. He even made it to the lintel above the front door. And Michael Card's song *El Shaddai* filled the under-construction rooms of our home as Emily's nimble fingers made Him dance up and down the piano keyboard. (Twenty years later Emily keeps this song practiced up knowing I want it played at the beginning and end of my memorial service.)

My love affair with *El Shaddai* was based initially on the reality that God would infuse my weakness with His strength, but I know now there's more. Our pastor, Bob Bonner, pointed out that the Hebrew root *shad* means breast.

God desires more than anything on earth to be our power source. As a nursing mother nourishes and calms a helpless babe, *El Shaddai* wants to nourish and calm us. As the mother is the infant's lifeline, God wants to be our lifeline. Cradled in God's arms is where we will find peace and calm. I understood the concept immediately having breastfed three daughters.

The stories of God Almighty went beyond the walls of the Squier home; our entire community knew that Mama Squier's power came from heaven above. As our circle of friends grew, inevitably first time visitors would inquire at the door, "Who is El Shadoo?" Invariably they'd stumble over His name. I loved listening to our daughters' explanations, "*El Shaddai* is the God who takes care of us." And when they grew older they'd add, "... when we realize we can't take care of ourselves." Yes, my daughters, you're getting it, and I pray it's a truth you remember everyday of your lives.

When the girls grew into adulthood and the physical demands of motherhood were no more, my life-sustaining relationship with *El Shaddai* changed. He became an old-friend whom I loved dearly, but smooth sailing dulled my dependency on Him. Not for long, however.

David and I had just returned home from our 40th anniversary cruise to the Scandinavian countries, and our daughter Elizabeth was eager to meet us for breakfast. In hand she held an ultrasound picture to confirm the news that she was pregnant. Her announcement was totally unexpected as was my response. Old fears, fears I thought Almighty God and I had conquered, pinned me to the mat: *What if this grand-baby arrives with my birth defect? I'll die if this baby's parents have to experience the pain that mine did.* On the heels of the fears came guilt. *I should be the last person on earth afraid of birth defects. Didn't I write a book about how God shows up, thanks to human brokenness?*

I prayed for the joy of the Lord, but the storm did not subside until the day I accompanied Elizabeth to her third trimester ultrasound appointment. Sheepishly I asked the perinatologist (an obstetrician who specializes in high-risk pregnancies) if he thought this child would inherit her grandma's birth defects. He looked at legless me seated in my wheelchair and repositioned himself at the machine-that-tells-all. Once again he scrutinized the babe in utero and confidently announced, "I see legs, I see knees and I see feet with toes." His words set this grandma free.

I recounted my emotional roller coaster to my 90-plus-year-old spiritual mom, Aunt Ginny, who had walked me through my first year of faith and prayed for me every day for thirty years until her dying day in 2009. "Aunt Ginny, does this battle never end? Fears that I thought were over are taking me down." Her tried and tested faith answered, "The battle gets more ferocious each year, Judy, but we win the battle each time our insufficiency drives us to the All-Sufficient God."

As my insufficiency drove me to *El Shaddai* during motherhood, yet again as a grandma I have found myself on His lap seeking the nourishment of truth and the comfort of His calming presence. Three grandbabies later, this leg-less Granny Goose knows where to hide out until the storm passes. Psalm 91 talks about *abiding in the shadow of the Almighty,* which I must again do as old fears of inadequa-cy can take me down. *Can a grandma without legs do all the things grandmas are supposed to do?* Indeed God Al-mighty, *El Shaddai,* squelches my unwarranted fears each time daughter Elizabeth tells me, "Your granddaughter Bri-anna woke up this morning and again the first thing she said was 'I miss Goose.'"

And I have to smile outwardly and inwardly when I re-member how one-year-old grandson Luka and I first con-nected. Being naturally shy, he stayed clear of the Goose until the day he discovered my stump. One morning as he walked by my wheelchair, my exposed stump caught his eye. Oh so cautiously he touched it, then went on by but came back later to touch it again. This marked his first self-ini-tiated contact with me, his grandma. *Thank You, Lord, for stumps.*

I think I get it now. We humans won't make the acquain-tance of *El Shaddai* when our self-confidence is stoked or our love tanks are full. We'll pass Him by when life is good. Success and prosperity cloud Him over, but it's in the rub-ble of our personal brokenness, our fears, our threatened dreams, when our faith gets cold feet, that we meet Him.

Brennan Manning has a unique blessing that I've heard him drop like an atom bomb at the end a talk. He credits it to his spiritual director, Larry Hine.

May your expectations be frustrated;
May your plans be thwarted;
May all your desires be withered into nothingness...
That you may experience the powerlessness
And poverty of a child and sing and
dance in the compassion of
God who is Father, Son and Holy Spirit.[17]

Brennan Manning gets it. We earthlings have strength and weakness backwards, don't we, Lord? We pray for smooth sailing thinking it will make us strong. Smooth sailing steers us away from *El Shaddai,* the only inexhaustible source of strength on earth. We think we are strong when we are strong, but the truth is we can only be strong when we are weak.

The apostle Paul got it and explained it in the New Testament in II Corinthians, chapter 12. Three times Paul had asked God to remove a thorn in his flesh. We aren't told what his physical ailment was, but we can tell it made him miserable. Miserable enough that Jesus Himself explained why His answer to Paul's triple plea was *no.* The secret of the ages is that power is perfected in weakness.

Because the words came from the mouth of the Lord Jesus Christ, Paul heard it and believed it and passed this hard-to-believe truth on to all future generations of the faith:

Once I heard that, I was glad to let it happen.
I quit focusing on the handicap and began appreciating

the gift. It was a case of Christ's strength moving
in on my weakness. Now I take limitations in stride,
and with good cheer, these limitations that cut me
down to size—abuse, accidents, opposition, bad
breaks. I just let Christ take over! And so the weaker
I get, the stronger I become.
(II Corinthians 12:9b-10 MSG)

I remember the first day I happened upon those verses. Flat on my back in the hospital with no strength for my upcoming master's comps and absolutely no energy to plan my wedding day just two weeks away, I read for the first time Paul's conclusion about true strength. My physical ailment identified with his, and I held on for dear life to *El Shaddai's* offer to be all that I needed. At that moment Paul's words became mine, and I let God Almighty turn my not-enough into His more-than-enough for two rites of passage – my career as a speech pathologist and my marriage to David Squier.

Yes, I get it, but it still boggles my mind to think that when *I am weak, then I am strong.* (II Corinthians 12:10b NASB) How can it be? Truly this is a truth that should be taught to our children and grandchildren along with the song "Jesus Loves Me." Don't you agree?

What About You?

Have you made peace with your inadequacies? I don't mean living in denial, pretending they don't exist. I mean knowing them by name and allowing them to escort you into the presence of *El Shaddai,* the All-Sufficient God.

But you say, "My inadequacies are hardly something I would talk about at a neighborhood block party." On the contrary, because I've never been able to hide my oh-so-obvious disability, I find myself talking about it more often than not. And guess what? Authentic honesty about where I'm weak provides an instant bond with total strangers and an automatic opener to where my strength lies.

Are you ready to trade that sinking feeling of inadequacy for *El Shaddai's* too-good-to-be-true offer? He invites you to throw away your mask of self-sufficiency, release the guilt and shame of your inadequacies and experience the relief that it doesn't depend on you! IT DOESN'T DEPEND ON YOU because the all-sufficiency of *El Shaddai* is yours.

> *I heard the Savior say,*
> *Thy strength indeed is small*
> *Child of weakness, watch and pray*
> *Find in Me thine all in all.*[18]

11

El Gibbor

MIGHTY WARRIOR

I'm Ready to Save Your Day.
May I?

I met *El Gibbor* when I hit the wall with my sixth set of artificial limbs. Getting new legs was always a fifty on my one to ten scale, so I'd reduce the stress with the following instruction: "Make the new legs exactly like my old ones. No new fangled technology for me!" Then came the day I weakened and signed up for new technology's promise of a better life. I let down my guard except for one request, "You decide what will work best for me, but make sure the new legs have praying knees." I wanted to guard my morning ritual of kneeling in prayer, but what I asked for and what I got were two different things.

Imagine my shock when the prosthetist presented my new legs with one stipulation: "This cosmetic covering is as close to real looking as you can get but it has one drawback. It will tear if you kneel and the replacement cost is $400 per leg." *DUH!*

Auf Wiedersehen, farewell to my morning practice of kneeling by the couch, looking out the window up into our

El Elyon pine trees, sipping my cup of coffee while talking to His Majesty. The prosthetist obviously ignored my request. Didn't he hear me when I said I wanted praying knees? Obviously not. But God heard me. In more ways than one, the new limbs would grow me a set of praying knees. Yes, indeed. I, the frustrated owner of a $40,000 pair of artificial limbs, would be growing some heavy-duty spiritual knees. *God, I'm stuck. Help!* would become my twenty-four hour cry for the next two years.

The problems began immediately. The fit on the right leg was never right; sitting down felt like skydiving as the new knees offered no resistance to this bilateral above-knee amputee. I felt like I was walking on springs and just standing up was treacherous. I presented the prosthetist with my carefully compiled list of seven things that weren't working for me. I told him everything. His heartless twofold response cut me off at the pass: "I don't know what you mean and, by the way, this is our last appointment; I'm moving to Idaho."

I hobbled out of the room on my lemon legs, sobbing hysterically, feeling unheard, without help or hope and with no battle plan or solution. That's the week I collapsed into *El Gibbor's* arms and clung to Him for dear life. He met me in Psalm 20 as the emotional shame of failure beat me to a pulp. I devoured the following words as He began to craft an unexpected pair of spiritual knees:

A David Psalm

GOD answer you on the day you crash,
The name God-of-Jacob put you out of harm's reach,
Send reinforcements from Holy Hill,
Dispatch from Zion fresh supplies,
Exclaim over your offerings,
Celebrate your sacrifices,
Give you what your heart desires,
Accomplish your plans.

When you win, we plan to raise the roof
and lead the parade with our banners.
May all your wishes come true!
That clinches it—help's coming,
an answer's on the way,
everything's going to work out.

See those people polishing their chariots,
and those others grooming their horses?
But we're making garlands for GOD our God.
The chariots will rust,
those horses pull up lame—
and we'll be on our feet, standing tall.

Make the king a winner, GOD;
the day we call, give us your answer.
(Psalm 20 MSG)

El Gibbor promised He would take full responsibility for my rescue. Knowing this gave my discouragement the boot. Like an athlete training for the Olympics, I gave mastering the legs my all, even taking two sets of limbs to Illinois that spring for my trip back to see Mom. Wearing the old, safe set I carried the loser legs in a huge duffle bag. On and off planes, on and off buses I went, the lady with four legs.

Judy and her four legs

As Mom walked inside the parallel bars in rehab, recovering from recent surgery, my new legs and I kept in step with her on the outside. The shared challenge of getting back on our feet gave us a unity of purpose for the first time in our lives. We commiserated. We laughed and had fun together. Fun together? Mom and me? *Thank You, Lord.*

But my practice did not make perfect. I tried to become a success story until one day my blatantly honest friend, Linda, said, "Judy, I think you have unrealistic hope." She'd known my steadiness with previous limbs and made this comment as she helped me to my car, "Judy, you had a death grip on my arm. You have no balance."

For two years my legs and I did the circuit – back to the orthopedist we went, then to a consultation with a new prosthetist, next a meeting with a team of prosthetists, followed by an appointment with a physical therapist. One step forward, ten steps back. I ended up with a hydraulic knee on the right leg and a pneumatic knee on the left. I was instructed to walk by moving my right stump forward while moving my left stump backward. My brain became befuddled. My nerves were frayed. I'd had it!

Further attempts to solve my walking problems triggered a balancing problem. I began to fall down with no warning and would find myself flat on my back while cooking in the kitchen, while pumping gas at a gas station, in a parking lot.

God, I can't do this.
YOU ARE SO RIGHT, MY CHILD.
God, I've tried everything and still no solution.
I WANT TO BE YOUR SOLUTION,
TRUST ME AND ONLY ME.

God blessed the day I awoke with the idea to track down my previous prosthetist who had crafted two sets of limbs that had worked. With a single phone call, I was talking to the receptionist I'd known a decade earlier. I learned that the prosthetist I liked, David, was no longer employed there, but prosthetist Bill was still there and was, in fact, the lead prosthetist. UGH! The one I'd vowed I'd never go back to. The insensitive one who had responded to my complaints about large thighs by saying, "I don't care if they are the size of garbage cans, as long as they work."

As I dug in my heels regarding scheduling an appointment with Bill, *El Gibbor* reiterated, "*I WANT TO BE YOUR SOLUTION, TRUST ME AND ONLY ME.*" Was I willing to let my Savior in heaven pick my savior on earth? Indeed, prosthetist Bill saved the day! Having worked with patients with birth defects like mine at San Francisco's Shriners Hospital, he understood immediately why I was stuck and made me a new set of legs just like the previous, old-fangled ones – and they worked!

No longer did it feel like I was walking on springs; no longer was I falling. My balance was steady. *El Gibbor* rescued me using the last person on earth I would have expected or chosen. I had a new song to sing: *You make me strong. God is bedrock under my feet, the castle in which I live, my rescuing knight.* (Psalm 18:2 MSG)

The circuitous route to a set of legs that worked seemed endless, but the day did finally come when once again I could kneel by the couch sipping my cup of coffee while talking to Jesus. And because of the delay, my spiritual knees mastered the discipline called praying without ceasing.

Truly *El Gibbor* saved the day, plus I learned the rewards of long delays. But I must confess I still catch myself opting for quick fixes. In fact, I overheard myself say just yesterday, "Being stuck is the pits."

"Will my flesh never get it?" I ask. "Probably not," I answer. But my spirit knows the truth. The honest to God truth is that though life's pits are the pits, we are never alone there. Someone precedes us there and is waiting to meet us there.

To think *El Gibbor,* this world's Mightiest Warrior, crawls down and enters our dank and dark places of defeat. He sets up camp there. Actually, He creates His throne room there. His mightiness replaces quaking knees with spiritual knees. And cold feet He transforms into feet that are willing to wait for Him no matter how long His rescue takes. He even performs heart surgery making our fainting hearts stouthearted.

And this is the promise that He sings to us in the waiting rooms of life – it's the verse Aunt Ginny gave me, the verse that I've clung to for half a century: *I will not in any way fail you nor give you up nor leave you without support. (I will) not, (I will) not, (I will) not in any degree leave you helpless nor forsake nor let (you) down, (relax My hold on you!) Assuredly not!* (Hebrews 13:5b AMP)

And ultimately His presence becomes the prize: *So we take comfort and are encouraged and confidently and boldly say, The Lord is my Helper; I will not be seized with alarm. I will not fear or dread or be terrified. What can man do to me?* (Hebrews 13:6 AMP)

WHAT ABOUT YOU?

Where are you stuck right now? I doubt the issue that's driving you crazy is artificial limbs that don't work. Maybe you are stuck with a neighbor who is harassing you or your children. Maybe you are grandparents who feel stuck raising grandkids, but you love them and want the best for them, so you won't even admit you are stuck. Are you stuck with an addiction? At dawn you vow you will not succumb to food, drink, drugs, pornography or shopping, but at night you collapse into bed defeated, feeling super-glued to this vicious cycle.

Maybe you or someone you love is one of thousands of candidates for a life-saving organ transplant list. Pastor Neil Smith and his wife Melanie never dreamt he'd be living with renal failure, nor could they have anticipated three half days per week being gobbled up by dialysis. But that's been their new normal for the past year and a half. Struck down are they, but not destroyed, as evidenced by their blessed periodic accounts of how *El Gibbor* their Mighty Warrior saves them from despair turning their unplanned waiting room into His throne room.

Melanie's November 9, 2012 e-mail was entitled "His Faithfulness Sings Over Us" and read as follows:

> *Who knew waiting could be so tiring? We*
> *want you to know though, as one of my*

dear hula sisters calls Him, the Chief Surgeon <u>was</u> and <u>is</u> still present. He's answering the entreaties you make on our behalf. In light of something I read this morning, we'd like you to add a request for a different kind of surgery; not for the recent fistula repair, but for our hearts . . . Neil's, mine, and ours, as a couple.

"When all kinds of trials and temptation crowd into your lives, my brothers and sisters, don't resent them as intruders, but welcome them as friends! Realize that they have come to test your faith and to produce in you the quality of endurance. But let the process go on until that endurance is fully developed, and you will find you have become men of mature character, men of integrity with no weak spots." (James 1:2-4 Phillips)

May we grow in welcoming Renal Failure as a "friend." He has not always been an easy fellow to embrace, especially since He has unabashedly brought along his accompanying pals – the siblings of the Limitations Family: Time, Energy, Strength, and Diet, as well as his best buddy, Dialysis.

Perhaps, after an initial, natural reaction of seeing them as intruders who have brought a life of "diminishing health and growing dependence," we want to call them "friends." We desire not to hinder the process that produces "endurance." May our loving Lord use them all in performing His transforming work of developing a Neil and Melanie of mature character with no weak spots . . . the kind in which He specializes . . . the kind He is committed to completing.

He is sooooo patient with us. We do still seek His will for a possible kidney transplant or regeneration, but above all else, we long for His resurrection life to be more deeply implanted in us. This is the real miracle.

Have a wonder filled day enjoying and pleasing Christ.

Melanie, for the two of us

Do we hear an "Hallelujah Chorus" here? And to think the same *El Gibbor* who rescues Neil and Melanie on a daily basis is on duty in our battlefields. But be forewarned – He doesn't promise to down your enemies with your first shout for help. In fact, you may grow hoarse as your *Help, Lord!* extends into weeks, months, years, possibly a lifetime. But He promises that as your dreams die, He will take their place, and as the Smiths' triumphant e-mail attests, His very presence makes the suffering worthwhile, producing a joy worth dying for.

12

Jehovah Jireh

THE LORD WILL PROVIDE

In Times of Need, I'm All You Need

My husband David and I always marveled at Father Abraham's rock-solid faith recorded in the book of Genesis in the Old Testament. When God told him to leave his familiar homeland, he was obedient. When God promised to make him the father of a mighty nation, Abraham believed Him, even though his wife Sarah was barren. For twenty-five long years they waited, until when Abraham was one hundred and Sarah was ninety, Isaac, their son of promise, was born.

Le Sacrifice d'Abraham [19]

But Abraham's supreme test came when God instructed him to sacrifice Isaac, the son of his great delight whose very name meant laughter. All the other tests paled in comparison to this one. Yet without an argument Abraham rose the next day; in fact, the Bible records that *he got up early.* He took everything but the sacrificial lamb. And when his son queried, "My father, where is the lamb for the burnt offering?" Abraham's faith responded with confidence, "God will provide for Himself the lamb." (Genesis 22:7-8 NASB)

By faith this father of the faith built an altar, tied his son to it and even lifted the knife for the deadly plunge when the angel of the Lord Himself stopped him. *Baa! Baa!* God provided a ram caught in a thicket by its horns. Abraham named the spot *Jehovah Jireh,* God will provide. Romans 4:20-21 tells us more about Abraham's exemplary faith. *Abraham never wavered in believing God's promise. In fact, his faith grew stronger, and in this he brought glory to God. He was fully convinced that God is able to do whatever he promises.* (NLT)

Indeed, Abraham's faith caught my husband's and my attention, so much so that we agreed early on if God gave us a son we would name him Abraham (despite the audible groans of our parents). Father Abraham's utter abandonment and prompt obedience to the will of his God more than qualified him for the title, the Father of our Faith. But what happens when we children of the faith find our faith falling short in mouse-sized challenges? What happens when we balk at the foot of our mount of testing and even turn a deaf ear to God? Come to find out, God does not abandon us. Instead, He meets us at the foot of our faith just as He met Abraham at the summit of his faithfulness.

Returning to Romania was never on my bucket list. Weren't my mind, emotions and will traumatized after that first mission trip in 2004? Romania's inaccessibility for me, a fulltime wheelchair user (I never took my artificial limbs on mission trips), pushed me miles outside my comfort zone. My frayed nerves calmed down once back in America thanks to plentiful ramps, curb cuts and wheelchair friendly public

Judy's *Jehovah Jireh* stories
from Romania [20]

places, until early one morning I sensed God hinting about a return trip to Romania. I dug in my heels. *Don't even mention it, God. I've done Romania once. I will never go back.*

I stood my ground until I recalled Jonah and realized his right to refusal landed him in the belly of a whale. Then came the morning I happened upon Psalm 119:32, which read, *I will not merely walk but run the way of your commandment when you give me a heart that is willing.* (AMP) Hesitantly I wrote "Romania" in the margin of my Bible. That's all God needed. That simple act provided a crack in my rock-solid refusal that was big enough for His little toe.

Autumn of 2004 found me minding my own business, out and about doing errands. As I drove, I listened to a book on tape, *Touch the Top of the World* by Erik Weihenmayer, the first blind mountain climber to ascend Mount Everest.[21] His daring-to-do-the-impossible awakened the only live-on-the- edge cell in my body, and I blurted out to my empty minivan, "I want to climb a mountain."

The Holy Spirit was quick, "How about Mount Romania?"

"Sign me up, Lord," was my caught-off-guard response.

In that instant my heart became willing, but my emotions refused to sign on the dotted line. My innards became divided. My fear of Romania's challenges waged war against my spirit's desire to trust God's faithfulness. What began as a low-grade dread catapulted into what I called an *internal hysteria*.

My cold feet watched as God put all of the pieces in place for the trip of His choosing, not mine. I knew it would be hard, and it was. Waking up that first morning back in the former KGB headquarters in Brashov, I faced the challenge of a flat tire on my wheelchair, the equivalent of an able-bodied person waking up to a broken leg.

My roommate Grace's gift of faith was ecstatic, "Yippee, God's going to do a miracle." My unbelief asked her great faith to leave the room.

Thankfully my zero faith didn't negate God's faithfulness, which showed up in a man named Cornel Dan Barbu and his boss, Daniel. Romania's two wheelchair experts just happened to be attending the 2005 Becky's Hope retreat. Within fifteen minutes I'd crowned them my wheelchair angels as they exchanged not one, but two worn-out tires with wheels that would never go flat. *O ye of little faith.*

We learned that the seventy-five Romanian moms were not scheduled to arrive for two days so our leadership team would be treated to a tour of the Romanian countryside. As our cars switchbacked higher and higher into the Carpathian Mountain range, I whispered, "Mount Romania. This is for You, Lord. I'm here for You."

Rounding the bend, my eyes beheld a cross at the summit. From that lone cross I could hear Jesus whispering, "Judy, this is for you. I'm here for you."

Faith the size of Father Abraham's welled up in my soul as I remembered the words of the old hymn "Higher Ground."

> *I'm pressing on the upward way,*
> *New heights I'm gaining every day;*
> *Still praying as I'm onward bound,*
> *"Lord, plant my feet on higher ground."*
>
> *My heart has no desire to stay,*
> *Where doubts arise and fears dismay;*
> *Though some may dwell where these abound,*
> *My prayer, my aim is higher ground.*[22]

Returning to the retreat headquarters for a glorious week of ministry, I shared my brokenness. In the midst of one talk, my deformed left hand popped up and preached a three-point sermon, surprising even me. The gateway to heaven flung open for each of us as my brokenness ventured out of hiding to set all of us free.

My spirit soared as the angelic voices of the moms, set free by God's truth, sang a favorite hymn of mine in their native tongue:

> *Long my imprisoned spirit lay,*
> *Fast bound in sin and nature's night.*
> *Thine eye diffused a quickening ray;*
> *I woke the dungeon flamed with light.*
> *My chains fell off, my heart was free,*
> *I rose, went forth, and followed Thee.*[23]

As I watched the chains of pain and shame fall off of the Romanian moms of disabled children, I sensed my chains falling off, too. But I would soon learn that more than chains fell that year. Returning to my America I had the following e-mail message awaiting me from Cristi Tepes, the man who drove us to the train station: "Judy, I heard your teaching and it was good, but what spoke louder to me was watching you crawl onto the train today. It was then that I saw Satan fall."

As the wheels of our plane touched down on the runway in San Francisco, I said to my roommate, "Gracie, we survived!"

Her quick response was, "Judy, we didn't just survive, we were victorious!"

Victorious? Didn't all of my kicking and screaming disqualify me from such an honorable title?

Judy and Grace – home from Romania

God answered, "No, My child. Your will opened the door wide enough for My little toe, remember?" And He added, "My beloved, it matters not whether you travel by foot, wings, wheels or stumps, I, your *Jehovah Jireh*, will provide and transport you to the High Places!"

Fortunately His provision is not dependent upon the speed of our obedience. His grace knows that obedience to His challenges comes harder for some than for others. For me, my faith grovels and groans before it grows. I'm embarrassed to admit the truth – kicking and screaming usually precede my *Yes, Lord*.

Oh, how my spirit longs for a humongous faith like Father Abraham's or the expectant faith of my roommate Gracie, who jumped with joy in anticipation of God's imminent miracle. But instead I live this life with my mustard-seed-sized flicker of faith that is met by my Big God's faithfulness. And each time He provides His heroic rescue I find myself plopped on His lap, slobbering my *Jehovah Jireh* with thank-filled kisses.

Meanwhile, my feeble faith strains to hear the songs of saints on higher ground. Suzanna is a modern day woman of rock-solid faith. She, like Father Abraham, was a senior citizen when her big test hit. Suzanna was rapidly going blind due to cataracts, which proved inoperable due to severe, uncontrolled glaucoma. Having no family in the area, she was asked by her counselor, Marian, "What will you do, Suzanna, when you can no longer see well enough to come and go, to cook your own meals safely, and care for yourself?"

Suzanna thought for a long moment, then with tears streaming down her face her faith answered, "I have known God since childhood when my Norwegian grandmother and Jamaican grandfather told me all the wonderful Bible stories. I have walked close beside God now for many, many years. I cannot say what I will do when that time comes, but I can say that I know God will provide a ram in the thicket."

The ram in the thicket. God's ace in the hole to rescue Father Abraham and his future descendants of the faith. God's ram in the thicket met Abraham and Isaac on Mt. Moriah, the same geographical site which 2,000 years later was called Golgotha, the same mountain where *Jehovah Jireh* provided the Lamb of God who came to take away the sin of the world. On the cross of crucifixion, God Himself was the sacrificial ram in the thicket.

I am smitten realizing God provided an escape hatch for Abraham and Isaac, but no way of escape did He provide for

Himself and His Son on Calvary. Jesus Christ, the Lamb of God set His face like flint to go to Jerusalem and ultimately to the mount of crucifixion. Why? God wanted more than anything to offer sinful man the privilege of jumping up onto His big-enough-for-all-of-us lap so that we could slobber Him with thankful kisses.

To bridge the great chasm between Holy God and sinful humanity, God's Son became the once and for all perfect sacrifice. He did His part and waits for us to do ours. God waits for us to accept His Son's sacrifice as our own. He waits for us to embrace Jesus as our very own ram in the thicket.

WHAT ABOUT YOU?

On what mountain do you wait today for God to provide?

A ram in the thicket means that *Jehovah Jireh* meets you in your peril and provides what's needed, no matter what the cost, even when it requires the death of God Himself as the only perfect sacrifice.

But some may be balking at the need of a sacrifice. *I'm a decent person, I haven't killed anybody,* you might be thinking. But God's standard of excellence is high – too high for me and too high for even you. Jesus said if we so much as think a harsh thought against another, we are murderers. And the sixth commandment says, *Thou shalt not murder.*

Maybe you have signed on the dotted line with modern day thinkers declaring, "God, You aren't the boss of me. There is no moral law regarding right and wrong. It's all relative." But what if they're wrong? What if you aren't the boss of the universe? What if a loving God created you for a purpose and wants to empower you to become all that you long to be? What if the only thing separating you from His love is your refusal to receive Him on His terms?

What are His terms, you ask?
- Admitting you need help
- Being willing to admit you need a Savior
- Receiving Jesus as that Savior, the innocent

Lamb of God who died in your place

Romans 8:32 nails it. *He who did not spare His own Son, but delivered Him over for us all, how will He not also with Him freely give us all things?* (NASB) Are you willing to personalize this promise as your very own? In so doing, your leap of faith means you are entrusting your future needs to *Jehovah Jireh,* the Lord who promises to provide you with all things free of charge.

13

Adonai

LORD AND MASTER

*The God Who Patiently Awaits
the Honor He is Due*

My number one goal growing up with a disability was independence. Oh the glory of being able to do *anything* unassisted. *All by myself* put a feather in my bonnet. Standing and walking on my own two feet – no matter that they were artificial – gave me dignity. Driving the family car gave me mobility and speed. Then came my teenage years working as a counselor at the camp for crippled children where I could actually assist others. Slowly but surely my artificial limbs and I sprouted the wings of independence.

I always knew I could fly. The question was how high? But then came the day this goose was shot out of the sky – the day I learned that God intends for His followers to live a life of dependence – dependence on Him. Week after week the altar inscription at Peninsula Bible Church in Palo Alto, California stared me in the face: *You are not your own for you have been bought with a price.* (I Corinthians 6:19-20 NASB) Then I learned from the Apostle Paul's letters in the New Testament that the goal in the Christian life is to surrender our rights to Jesus Christ. Oswald Chambers, in his ageless devotional *My Utmost for His Highest*, finally nailed it for me: "Beware of refusing to go to the funeral of your independence."[24]

Becoming a Christian involves inviting Jesus Christ to become our Savior, but also our Lord. Looking back I see that accepting the Savior's offer to save me came easy, but surrendering my will to the Lord has been a lifelong challenge. *You mean, God, You want to be the Boss of me? But You see how hard it is for me to let my husband choose the parking spot.*

One Christmas, my three Jim Shore figurines perched on the mantle (a shepherd, a donkey and a lamb) had the nerve to ask me, "Judy, which one are you? Are you the donkey or the lamb?" Was I the strong-willed jack-ass demanding my rights or the sacrificial lamb surrendering my will to the Good Shepherd? *Ouch.*

I've been transparent about my struggle to let God lead, openly admitting my shortcomings. My authentic honesty got me into trouble one year, actually resulting in my being disinvited from teaching my Names of God series at the Christian high school our daughters attended. I'd already taught about *Elohim*, the Awesome Creator, and *El Shaddai*, the All-Sufficient God, and was scheduled to speak at the weekly girls' assembly for the next six weeks.

Looking out at the room full of teenage girls and their teachers I said: "*Adonai* is God's Hebrew name that means Lord and Master. God owns us and wants to be the Boss of our lives." I then let the cat out of the bag when I added, "This name is a hard one for me since I often prefer to do things my way." I was shocked to receive a phone call that evening from the lead teacher indicating a decision had been made to end my Names of God series.

Lordship. What does it take to let go and let God?

God heard my question and had an answer in response to my heart's cry. Three mission trips to Romania, plus one to Thailand, plus one to Brazil secured for me a limo-ride to the funeral of my independence.

Pastor Carol's postscript to our first Romania mission trip was, "Judy, you walked in obedience. No, you rolled in obedience. Well, to be more precise you crawled in obedience!"

"I did? Is that what Lordship is?"

"Yes, that's what Lordship is," my traveling companion Grace answered as we headed back home from our second mission trip to Romania. Then she added, "Remember, Judy, I wrote a song describing Lordship so you can't forget what it means:"

My Adonai

My Lord, my Master, I surrender to You.
My Lord, my Master, my Adonai.
My Lord, my Master, I surrender to You.

My Lord, my Master, my Adonai.

So many times I've fought You
Wanting to be in control.
So many times I've hurt You, my Adonai.
But willingly I come now
I surrender my control.
Willingly to serve now, my Adonai, my Adonai.
When I let go of my will then
I see You everywhere.
When I let go I am free then, my Adonai
I want to see You smile at me
'Cause I am in Your will.
I want You to be pleased with me, my Adonai.[25]

That's the victorious note I'd wanted to end that second mission trip on – *Judy fully surrendered to Adonai.*

Instead, as the wheels of our jumbo jet touched down on the runway in San Francisco, unbeknownst to me, I would resume life as normal – living in my own strength. As my wheelchair tires rolled up the accessible jet way to my America, as I had my independence back, Can-Do Judy kicked in. The pressure was off and instantly I reveled in the accessibility of home sweet home. Unconsciously I said *adios* to Jesus; *Adonai* became an Add On.

That was the year I learned how rigorous is the battle to maintain a yielded life, especially on those stress-free days when we believe that we can manage life on our own. Thanks to that second trip to Romania, I discovered what it is that makes Jesus smile: Jesus smiles when we invite Him into our ordinary, Can-Do Days, not so much because we need Him, but because deep down we realize that apart from Him we can do nothing.

By mission trip number three I was confident that *Adonai* and I were on the same page. By then my "Not I's" had become "Aye, Aye Sirs" – even in 110 degree Bucharest temperatures, even with no accessible bathrooms, even when my creature comforts boiled down to one lopsided fan. As the trip ended, as David (this time my traveling companion) and I collapsed into the cushy seats of our Boeing 777, my spirit soared. We'd not just finished the course, we had finished strong.

Little did I know as our plane descended onto American soil, the trip's biggest challenge was ahead for me. God had some unfinished business from trip number two. He had an appointment with Can-Do Judy. Horror of horrors! My wheelchair was lost.

Judy missing her lost wheelchair

I sang no alleluias that first night as David carried me from the car into our home nor as I crawled from room to room. *Does no good deed go unpunished, Lord? Didn't the Squiers just deliver two hun-*

dred wheelchairs with Wheels for the World so Romanians need no longer crawl? As my dear husband carried me, as I crawled, as we drove to San Francisco International Airport the next morning to see if my wheelchair had arrived, *Adonai* had the stage set for some big growth.

While David went inside to the United Airlines lost and found, Agitated Judy drove our minivan around the airport loop. *Will the chair be there? What if it isn't there?*

In the emotional wrestling match I heard a still, small voice. "Am I enough? Am I enough?"

"What?" I growled. "If that's You, God, You know Can-Do Judy can't do life without her wheelchair!"

As I circled for the seventh time, knowing I had nowhere else to go, I finally let go to God. As my steel will yielded to His, Can-Do Judy crawled up on the altar of sacrifice so that when David plus wheelchair appeared at the curb, I knew *Adonai* was not an Add On.

Kicking and screaming at first, then finally surrendering all, my life became a living and holy sacrifice.

> *Therefore I urge you, brethren,*
> *by the mercies of God, to present your bodies*
> *a living and holy sacrifice, acceptable to God,*
> *which is your spiritual service of worship.*
> (Romans 12:1 NASB)

My friend Betty Bloomer performed such a spiritual service of worship each morning refusing to get out of bed until her will was totally surrendered to *Adonai*. Only when each renegade thought and each stubborn emotion were in the coffin would she begin a new day yielded wholly to her Master. Some days my mentor-in-Lordship would relay on the telephone, "Judy, the battle raged this morning for forty-five minutes before I experienced the sweet surrender."

Daughter Emily, having completed her three thousand hours of supervised counseling, recently took on the challenge of two national licensing exams. I cried along with her when she phoned to say she had flunked the first exam by one point. But fifteen minutes later came another call. "Mom, I'm okay. I just remembered a devotion I read last night from *Streams in the Desert*: "Submission to the divine will is the softest pillow on which to recline."[26]

How great the relief when our whitened knuckles finally release their grip so we can collapse onto *Adonai's* pillow of peace knowing He's got everything under control and He is worthy of our trust.

WHAT ABOUT YOU?

Who's the boss of you? Have you met *Adonai*, or do you pride yourself in being the master of your fate and the captain of your soul?

Richard Scarry's *Pig Will and Pig Won't* children's book is a Squier family favorite. Not just a book on manners, for me it cuts to the quick. Is my will surrendered or defiant? Either I will or I won't. I grieve to think how often I begin my day promising *Adonai* that I will, but throughout the day Can-Do Judy decides I won't.

The issue of Lordship is no laughing matter. *Lord, please rescue me from the deadly, momentary pleasure of doing things my own way.* Could that be the prayer of your heart today?

Frank Sinatra is remembered for his signature song, "I Did It My Way." My flesh loves the song, but my spirit more and more loves reclining on the soft pillow of surrendering to *Adonai.* So I'm memorizing Grace Rhie's song to keep my will set like flint on my spirit's goal.

> *My Lord, my Master, I surrender to You.*
> *My Lord, my Master, my Adonai.*
> *My Lord, my Master, I surrender to You.*
> *My Lord, my Master, my Adonai.*

Are you ready to join the happy song? Is your will willing to surrender to the God who owns you? Making Him your Lord is step number one when you become a Christian. But it's so much more than that. Daily time in Bible study and prayer is the next step along with ongoing fellowship with other believers. But it's even more than that. It's a moment-by-moment relationship with the God of the universe whose Son smiles when we invite Him into our ordinary CanDo Days, not so much because we need Him but because we finally realize that apart from Him we can do nothing. I'm all for making Jesus smile. Will you join me?

14

Adonai Tsuri

THE LORD MY ROCK

The Rock-Solid God Who Makes Us Unshakeable

I remember the Monday morning I was digging out from under the mounds of laundry after the Squier family's too full and too fast weekend. The girls were at school as their mom joylessly sorted through the dirty jeans, the grass-stained sports uniforms, the sheets for five beds. Obviously it would be a long day. Far from my mind was the devotion I'd read at 5:00 a.m. about Jesus being the Rock. Sadly enough, this Christian woman had hit rock bottom and it wasn't even 9:00 a.m.

"Hello, anybody home?" a cheerful voice interrupted my battle-weariness. Grabbing my cane, I cautiously navigated my artificial limbs through the soiled mounds, down the hall to find my friend Mary peeking her head in the front door. We exchanged a hug, some small talk and then she handed me a small, ornate container. Her enthusiasm burst into my doldrums. "My Dad just got back from Gibraltar, Spain, and he brought this home for you. It's a little piece of the Rock of Gibraltar. He calls you his walking Rock of Gibraltar."

My curiosity caused me to hurry past the faux-jeweled

container to examine the contents. Lifting the lid I saw much more than the jagged one and one-half inch stone inside. Mary's father's vote of confidence infused my faint heart with a limestone strength akin to the 1400-foot-high rock bordering Spain.

No longer did I feel buried under the heap as I returned to the laundry room. The Rock of Gibraltar in my pocket had pole vaulted me to the Rock that was higher than I. Thoughts of Mary's dad turned to memories of my own dad who had gone to heaven two years earlier. Oh how he loved to quote that verse in Psalm 61 – *Lead me to the Rock that is higher than I.* And, oh, how he loved a challenge. He'd choose the rugged, uphill grind any day, whereas my pick would be smooth terrain dotted with shade trees and a tea garden at the trail's end.

Despite my preference for the easy road, my father's faith was definitely a major stepping stone for me to Jesus, the Rock. Aunt Ginny's explanation of a personal relationship with Christ at a time when my life had hit rock bottom further connected me to the Son of God as the necessary, but too often overlooked Cornerstone of the Christian life.

With nearly fifty years of marriage to David Squier, it's obvious who the true Rock of Gibraltar is in our family. His solid, unemotional faith, plus his unconditional love are a daily stepping stone so I can see what Christlikeness looks like. David walks the walk while Judy talks the talk, though I must admit there are days when I wish the dear man showed more emotion. I conveyed that to a friend one morning over coffee and was set straight by her wise rebuke. "Judy, David is a rock and rocks don't get excited." *Thank You, Lord, that my husband is a rock.*

Rocky terrains, gravel driveways, sandy beaches, and cobblestones have never been my friends, whether I was walking or riding in a wheelchair. I like to look at a garden with stepping stones, but for my artificial limbs to actually walk on them was a challenge I'd avoid. Then came the day, after I'd retired all seven sets of prostheses at age 60, that I acquired my very own stepping stone.

A well-intentioned woman from the audience at a Christian Women's Club talk excitedly invited me to follow her to the parking lot where she opened the trunk of her car filled with a dozen multi-colored mosaic cement squares. "They're stepping stones," she explained. "I make them, and I want you to have one." Her excitement was contagious as I took great care in choosing the stone with a big red star.

I thanked her profusely for her gift but just had to voice my confusion to my traveling companion and swimming buddy, Froggy, on the drive home. "Did that lady not notice I have no legs? Why would I need a stepping stone?"

It was God who quieted my query with this explanation, "Consider her gift a supreme compliment, not a stumbling block. She saw beyond what others see. She saw your spiritual limbs."

Reading Scripture for the past half century, I conclude that God has a special place in His heart for stones of all sizes, using them to give special height and might to pebble-sized people. I think of the shepherd-boy David and his five smooth stones, only one of which was needed to down the 9-foot, 9-inches tall Goliath. I smile when I remember how my friend Rusty, a trial lawyer, made a habit of carrying five stones into the courtroom, his tangible reminder to trust in the Rock that is higher than I.

I learned of another famous stone in the Bible when my friend Jeff complimented me on my book *His Majesty in Brokenness*. "Thanks for raising your Ebenezer when you wrote your book."

"Raising my what?" I asked.

He explained how in I Samuel 7, when God's people experienced His rescue from the Philistines, they raised their Rock of Help called an Ebenezer stone. Ebenezer stones are concrete reminders of God's faithfulness.

Joni Eareckson Tada identifies her Ebenezer as follows: "My wheelchair is my Ebenezer. I've raised it up as a memorial to commemorate God's grace in my life. It reminds me, and everyone who sees me smile in it, that God is my help."[27]

"What actually is an Ebenezer stone?" I asked myself one day. My conclusion: An Ebenezer stone is a rock hewn in a soul that testifies: *He (God) brought me up out of the pit of destruction, out of the miry clay; and He set my feet upon a rock making my footsteps firm.* (Psalm 40:2 NASB)

An Ebenezer stone is born when we find *Adonai Tsuri* in our pit of destruction and give Him permission to make something beautiful. Peering back at my pit, I raise my Ebenezer stones to pay homage to the One Who plucked me out of that pit. My orthopedic shoe, once dowdy, but now dazzling with gold proves that God uses what pains us for His Masterpiece; my deformed-from-birth left hand pops out of hiding to testify that He makes a sermon out of what shames us. My three-fingered left hand packs a punch with its three-point sermon. And the very life of this old lady with no legs shouts, "Everything from God, nothing from me."

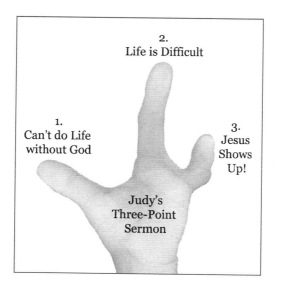

Ebenezer stones are all around us for those who have eyes to see. Be forewarned, you won't find them in the high and mighty, self-reliant crowd. Heaven calls that fool's gold. Ebenezer stones are hammered out among humble souls who recognize that Rock of Gibraltar strength comes not from within, but from acknowledging that without the Rock of Ages we can do nothing.

WHAT ABOUT YOU?

Are you in the pebble-sized people crowd? Believe it or not, admitting you are feeble and frail is the first step in becoming a walking (or wheeling) Rock of Gibraltar. Sure, we can fake it and pump out a more-than-conqueror demeanor, but what happens when that fizzles as early as 9:00 a.m.?

If you're like me, your daily goal is to avoid rocky terrain at all costs. But in heaven's eyes, rock-hard challenges are potential stepping stones to Jesus. He wants to meet us where we're stuck. Actually being stuck may mean we have slowed down enough for Him to get our attention.

Are you ready to trade in your pint-sized pebble for an Ebenezer stone? Have you discovered it yet? If not, then ask God to open your eyes to see how He is your Rock of Help. Then add your voice to mine and together let's sing the chorus to an old hymn to confirm that *Adonai Tsuri* is our personal Rock.

The Solid Rock

My hope is built on nothing less
Than Jesus' blood and righteousness
I dare not trust the sweetest frame
But wholly lean on Jesus' name

On Christ the solid Rock I stand

All other ground is sinking sand
All other ground is sinking sand.[28]

One more thought – as you reflect on Christ, your Solid Rock, you may also want to think about the people God has used in your life as stepping stones to Himself. A parent or grandparent? An aunt maybe? A teacher or an acquaintance who leans on the Rock? Why not bless them with an unexpected note or phone call to thank them for their role in introducing you to Jesus, your very own Rock of strength and stability!

15

Jehovah Rapha

THE GOD WHO HEALS

*The Healer God Who Makes
All Suffering Worth It*

B eing born broken surely set the stage for me to realize I needed a healer. Growing up in the church, I accumulated much information about how Jesus, the Son of God, healed broken people, but it took decades before I made the connection between the Healer and me.

I don't recall spotting *Jehovah Rapha* on duty during my many hospitalizations at Shriners. No one but the anesthesiologist greeted me when my gurney arrived in the green operating room. The visitor's chair by my bed was usually empty. And I never saw *Jehovah Rapha* amongst the white-starched coats during Monday morning doctor rounds. It wasn't until I was sixty-six years old that I learned, beyond a shadow of a doubt, He was on duty all along.

"You're going to love this hospital, Dear," David told me when he phoned after his intake procedure for treatment for his prostate cancer.

"Why will I love it?" I asked curiously.

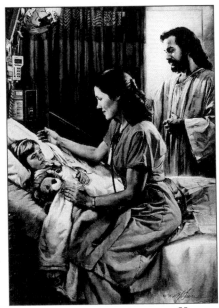

The Comforter by Nathan Greene [29]

"Because Jesus is everywhere."

The hospital lobby at Loma Linda University Medical Center was the first place he took me when we arrived for his three months of outpatient proton therapy. He was right. Jesus was everywhere, thanks to the framed paintings by Nathan Greene. One picture showed Jesus, the Great Physician, overseeing surgery in an operating room. Another art piece showed Jesus standing at the bedside of a little girl. Jesus and me, I thought. And then there was Jesus present with a family during a doctor's appointment.

Somehow His presence in the paintings photoshopped Him into my memories of hospitalizations over half a century earlier. *You were with me all along, weren't You, Lord?*

As David and I introduced ourselves at the new patient orientation I spoke with deep emotion. "I'm grateful for my husband's cancer because it's in coming to Loma Linda I finally can see that Jesus was with me 24/7 during my many hospitalizations growing up."

To this day I have the little red spiral notebook that contains my innermost thoughts the night before the long-awaited surgery enabling me to wear artificial limbs:

Tomorrow I go to surgery. Don-Don-Don-Don.

With no platform to voice my fears, journaling became a road to healing even as early as age ten. My little notebook shares the shelf with twenty-five other journals packed to the gills with fears and frustrations that were ultimately met by a healing God.

Writing has been a God-given tool to help me process life and to aid me in understanding myself and others. Eventually my journals were christened, "My Pit to Praise" books, as I would record a festering problem, wait for God's response and then praise Him as my listening heart received His thoughts and solutions. My books contain story after story of God's healing work in emotionally-broken Judy.

A frequently asked question by readers has been, "You talk a lot about your father, but can you tell us more about your relationship with your mother?" My unpublished journals could tell you all you'd ever want to know and more.

The truth be told, Mom and I were never close. I know it broke her heart when I was born with incomplete legs and a webbed hand. Repeated hospitalizations and corrective surgeries thwarted emotional bonding since visiting hours at Shriners were restricted to three hours on Sundays. Parents were not even allowed to be with their child the day of surgery.

Mom's and my emotional distance continued on into

my adulthood when marriage and a career moved me two thousand miles away. But Mom was promoted to hero status when she came out to help after each of our daughters was born. She was the expert, and I had a teachable spirit.

After Dad died, Mom stayed in Illinois, eventually moving in with my sister. As Mom's health waned, my trips from the West Coast to the Midwest increased. I remember the time one ten-day visit was ending when she took a turn for the worse. Awaking in my makeshift bed (two upholstered chairs face to face work fine when you don't have legs) as near to her bed as possible, I sensed an urgency to stay longer.

I can still hear the silent argument I had with God regarding the importance of my getting back home to San Francisco and to my family. I can still feel the flood of joy when I decided to cancel everything for Mom. My choice opened the way for God to get down to business in building the relationship we'd never had.

Mom's growing health needs catapulted us into the realm of doctor's offices, hospitals, rehab centers – my old stumping ground. With six surgeries before I turned sixteen, I felt as much in my element in the hospital as plaster of Paris in a cast room.

Automatically, I functioned as Mom's advocate, her cheerleader and her friend. "Mom, you're doing great!" My heartfelt words applauded this 89-year-old woman standing in the hospital's parallel bars with perspiration dotting her forehead. I fell in love with my dear Mom as I watched her frail, one hundred pound body straining to walk in a pair of clunky moon boots.

Day after day I cheered Mom on – not jumping in the air, but sitting in my own wheelchair in my sixth set of artificial limbs, the nemesis set that I just couldn't master. As I watched Mom muster her might to walk, I found myself up on my feet. As Mom walked, I walked. I shadowed everything the physical therapist asked her to do.

Judy and Mom

When therapy was over, we'd drop into our wheelchairs, pooped but pleased. We'd roll side by side, or sometimes, propelling my chair with one hand, I'd push her chair from behind down the long hallway to Room 534A. Nurses, patients and passersby smiled. Everyone knew we were the mother-daughter team.

Unfinished business, called building a relationship, was in progress. We held hands. We recited Psalm 23. We prayed the Lord's Prayer. We wrote letters. We telephoned friends and relatives. We laughed as I protected her when the mighty, ninety-pound dietician marched in to give the all-too-familiar lecture about wise eating and Mom's need to gain weight.

Meanwhile, God built a set of parallel bars across the

chasm between us. Our togetherness in the present over-flowed to the separation in our past. Somehow my being there with Mom mysteriously translated into Mom being there with me fifty years earlier. It didn't matter which one of us was in the bed or which one was in the chair beside the bed. We didn't talk about it, nor did we analyze what was happening. We simply savored it.

Savoring the sweetness of a newfound friendship with Mom extended beyond the experience and beyond Mom's death one month after her ninetieth birthday. Again and again I have marveled at the bond of healing that developed just in the nick of time. Recently, after I'd related the ac-count of our almost-missed relationship, an acquaintance responded, "What fascinates me, Judy, is that instead of growing bitter in your lonely hospitalizations, you became a cheerleader, even without a role model."

"How could that be?" we pondered.

Then one day I understood. When God gets down to business, He doesn't just build a bridge across a great chasm. He fills the chasm with Himself. Jesus was there for me be-side the anesthesiologist in the green room. He was seated in the empty chair next to my many hospital beds day and night sharing the seat with my parents for three hours on Sundays. And *Jehovah Rapha* was not just standing in the crowd of doctors, but He was enlightening them on Monday mornings as they made their rounds.

Jesus cheering me on provided the perfect role model so that I could give to Mom what she wasn't permitted to give to me. Indeed, Mom's illnesses and my participation in her care set the stage for us to revisit a place of separation, enabling us to walk through it together.

Thanks to Loma Linda and Nathan Greene's true-to-life art, I see now that *Jehovah Rapha* walks the halls of hospitals and clinics and doctors' offices. He is more than the Great Physician; He is the cure. When He doesn't heal our broken pieces, He inhabits us, changing us from the inside out so that we can become wounded healers. Our healing touch is not our own, but it is the touch of God extended to the next wounded soul.

How ironic that God's healing, rescuing touch was withheld one black Friday centuries ago when a Man of Sorrows was nailed to an old rugged cross. Surely heaven's angels stomped their feet as the *Jehovah Rapha* Himself was ripped, torn and crushed. And to think *it was our pains he carried—our disfigurements, all the things wrong with us.* (Isaiah 53:4 MSG)

I will forever remember a comment made by Nick Palermo, the founder of the Capernaum Project branch of Young Life. "Picture Jesus bearing your brokenness on the cross; picture Jesus in a wheelchair on the cross."

As a fairly new leader with Young Life, Nick's first group contained someone with a disability. A special program for teens with disabilities developed one step at a time. He tells about his first experience taking those teens to a Young Life Camp. The stop at a fast food restaurant on the way was anything but fast, meaning their arrival to camp was much later than planned. After getting each of them out of the van and into the cabin, novice Nick was responsible for getting each one into bed. Not an easy assignment.

After what seemed like hours, he finally turned off the lights and sighed an exhausted sigh of relief as he climbed the ladder to his top bunk. As his head hit the pillow, as he tasted the joy of a good night's sleep, he heard one of the boy's calling, "Nick, Nick..."

"What?" he growled.

"You need to turn me."

Begrudgingly he descended the ladder and walked across the room to reposition the boy. As he made his way back up the ladder, looking out the window he saw a full moon and heard Jesus say, "Nick, it was Me you just turned."

Jesus Himself said: I'm telling the solemn truth: Whenever you did one of these things to someone overlooked or ignored, that was me—you did it to me. (Matthew 25:40 MSG)

WHAT ABOUT YOU?

Mother Teresa spoke of Jesus disguising Himself in the poorest of the poor. I extend that to Jesus disguising Himself in our personal pain and shame, the very things we pray for Him to eliminate. People have found Him in the midst of their unstoppable pain, brain tumors, breast cancer, Alzheimer's, ADD, ADHD, addictions, botched surgery, macular degeneration, IBS, allergies, aging, obesity, depression, suicidal tendencies – to name a few. And He's waiting to be found in all the other human suffering that I failed to mention.

Could it be that suffering is God's amazing grace in disguise? It's in the pit of suffering that we realize we need Him, and that's where most of us first meet Him. I've said again and again that I doubt I'd have become a Christian if I had long, strong legs instead of stumps.

Jehovah Rapha's healing style is unique and beyond our human understanding. How can He heal using a degenerative disease, the sudden death of a loved one, the humiliation of bankruptcy or a future behind prisonbars? You just have to carry Isaiah 55:8-9 in your back pocket, *"My thoughts are nothing like your thoughts,"* says the LORD. *"And my ways are far beyond anything you could imagine. For just as the heavens are higher than the earth, so my ways are higher than your ways and my thoughts higher than your thoughts."* (NLT)

Beyond my understanding is a husband and wife team struggling to hold on as the husband copes with excruciating pain. Husband Terry just lost his job so they have no health insurance, and they fall through the cracks for hardship case medical care.

When wife Donna came to clean my house last week, I asked her how she was doing. Bursting into tears, she dropped to her knees in front of my wheelchair, put her head on my meager lap, and gave me a mile-long hug, sobbing the whole time. As she stood up to compose herself she said, "I just had to have a stump hug. I knew that that was the closest I could get to God's healing feet today."

A wise woman. Not only did she get it right that God is the Healer of life's pain, but she recognized the deeper truth that Jesus disguises Himself in human brokenness. Embracing brokenness took her miles up the mountain of healing. I ask myself and I ask you, what brokenness do we need to hug today?

One last thought: *Jehovah Rapha* does not turn us away because of lack of money, and He won't deny care for a pre-existing condition. Actually, He waits outside the door of our life's pain, longing to be invited in.

You ask, "What is His specialty?"

His answer, "I can cure all aches, all addictions and diseases, including willfulness, broken hearts, broken lives, broken families. My specialty is hopeless cases."

You ask, "What does He charge?"

He wants you to know that it's been paid in full on an old rugged cross. Then He adds, "At times, My healing may involve the infliction of physical, financial, emotional or social pain so that you may know the greater healing of your sin sick souls."

"When can treatment begin?" you ask.

"The minute you hand over the broken pieces and entrust yourself to My care," the Great Physician answers.

16

Jehovah Shalom

THE LORD IS PEACE

*The God Who Calms Our
Storms Inside and Out*

I've lost count how many times someone from an audience
has come up to me after I've given a speech, leaned in close
and said, "You've earned a medal for bravery, Honey."

Their comment is always a surprise since I've come to
know myself as a Much Afraid, never a Brave Heart. So my
answer to them goes something like, "Brave? Are you kidding? God knows I'm a sissy." And then I point my finger
heavenward and add my secret, "My God is big!"

Early childhood pictures prove that this girl isn't a can-
didate for a medal of bravery. Further proof, if needed, is my
friendship with 365 anti-fear Bible verses, one for each day
of the year. My Bible has them highlighted for instant and
constant reference.

Gideon is the one I think of when someone categorizes
me as brave. Wasn't he a sissy? Why else was he thrashing
wheat in a winepress instead of doing his work out in the
field? Yet sissy is not the label the Lord gave him. *The angel
of the Lord appeared to him and said: "The Lord is with*

you, O valiant warrior." (Judges 6:12 NASB)

God not only saw the man He created Gideon to be, but He infused him with all that was needed for him to become that man. In God's strength alone this no-longer-sissy risked his life, tearing down the town's altars of Baal, and with his meager three hundred men he won the battle against an estimated 135,000. My conclusion: God meets us where we are, even if He has to come a huntin'. He gives us what we lack – be it courage, skill or strength – to make us valiant warriors, and we worship Him. *And Gideon built an altar to the LORD there and named it Yahweh-Shalom.* (Judges 6:24 NLT) Gideon was a changed man because of his encounter with The Lord is Peace.

I remember pulling a Gideon myself during final week in college. *Jehovah Shalom* found me hiding out in the stacks at the University of Illinois library, quaking in my boots as I tried to prepare for five fearsome finals. That was the day this fairly new Christian happened upon a verse in Habakkuk 3:19. *The Lord God is my strength, my personal bravery and my invincible army; He makes my feet like hind's feet, and will make me to walk (not to stand still in terror, but to walk) and make (spiritual) progress upon my high places (of trouble, suffering or responsibility)!* (AMP)

Suddenly this sissy became a valiant warrior as that verse became indelibly imprinted on my soul. No longer cowering in my wheelchair, my emotions felt like the Lone Ranger seated high atop his white stallion. I could even hear the William Tell Overture in the background as God in me shouted, "Hi Ho, Silver! Away!"

True Peace

My brother-in-law, Pastor Paul, described *shalom* as follows in a sermon: a sense of wholeness, wellbeing, good relationships, and inner peace – the sweet spot. Surely these are characteristics that we all long for and characteristics that don't last long. Poof! Suddenly something or someone (maybe that someone is you or me) disturbs that delicate *sweet spot* so that once again we are striving after peace – peace of mind, peace in a relationship, peace in life's storms.

Most of us picture *shalom* as someone lounging by a pool sipping a chilled drink, basking in a no-stress zone. Instead, fables tell us that the peace prize went to the artist who depicted a bird atop her nest adjacent to a roaring waterfall. True peace is found in the midst of the storm. Birds know the secret.

Since childhood I have loved Elizabeth Cheney's insightful little poem, "Overheard in an Orchard:"

> *Said the robin to the sparrow*
> *"I should surely like to know*

Why these anxious human beings
Rush about and worry so."
Said the sparrow to the robin
"Friend, I think that it must be
That they have no Heavenly Father
Such as cares for you and me."[30]

More and more my spirit is calmed by God's fine-feathered friends. Seagulls have come to my rescue more than once as I've waited in the parking lot while David and the girls took a beach walk. One day as I sat in our minivan feeling that too familiar ache of being left behind, lonely Judy watched a lonely sea gull riding the wind. That's when *Elohim's* creative idea kicked in. I grabbed the girls' uneaten sandwich crusts, lowered the car window and started throwing crumbs into the air. Suddenly that lonely gull and lonely Judy were no longer alone. From then on the Squier family trips to the Pacific Coast included Mom's stash of leftover buns, bagels and tortillas. My beachcombin' family could always spot our car, the one engulfed by a cloud cover of squawking seagulls.

Then came the day when my love of birds became a love of feathers. It was the year God and David decided it would be prudent to sell our California home and retire to Oregon. A gloom cloud settled over my heart as David and I met with realtors, scheduled necessary improvements to our property, and watched strangers go to work, transforming our home of thirty years into a place I no longer recognized.

JEHOVAH SHALOM: THE LORD IS PEACE

That's when *Jehovah Shalom* started dropping peace feathers in unexpected places along my path. First, one appeared on the floor of the realtor's office. Another appeared on the driveway of our soon-to-be-sold home and another in our bedroom in Oregon. Each feather conveyed a simple reminder – *Peace be still.* And each humble feather accomplished its work as I would lean down from my wheelchair, pick it up and cradle it in my hand. Looking heavenward, my ever-increasing inner peace would whisper, *Thank You, Lord.*

Daughter Emily inherited her mom's love of birds and feathers. We delight in our exchange of unique bird cards with at least one feather glued on the front. And Emily is discovering a tried and true way to calm one's soul through Scripture memorization. She found a winner in Matthew 6:26 in *The Message. Look at the birds, free and unfettered, not tied down to a job description, careless in the care of God. And you count far more to him than birds.*

The *Jehovah Shalom* who visited Gideon centuries ago came to earth as Jesus of Nazareth. Though His life was characterized by much unrest, He brought peace to many a troubled soul, earning Him the title Prince of Peace. In Mark 4:35-41, His disciples roused the sleeping Son of God as waves poured into their boat, threatening to sink it. *He told the wind to pipe down and said to the sea, "Quiet! Settle down!" The wind ran out of breath; the sea became smooth as glass.* (MSG) And even the waves of a stormy sea obeyed Him.

Our Prince of Peace doesn't just calm a raging sea from His pillow inside the boat, He calms His distraught disciples both in Bible times and in our times. And when our fears run out of breath, He invites us to take a stroll with Him. The song "Strollin' on the Water" is a favorite of another friend, Terry, who has been a quadriplegic for four decades. As he belts out the song of his heart, I can feel the wild waves dousing our wheelchairs, and I can see his paralyzed hand holding on for dear life to *Shalom's* nail-scarred hand.

Surely Horatio Spafford faced a stormy emotional sea as he boarded an ocean liner and traveled to the spot where the Atlantic had swallowed his four precious daughters. After the captain pointed out the probable location, this bereaved dad went down to his cabin and composed the hymn that one hundred and forty years later brings peace to many a troubled soul.

When peace, like a river, attendeth my way,
When sorrows like sea billows roll
Whatever my lot, Thou hast taught me to say,
It is well, it is well with my soul.[31]

What About You?

Is it well with your soul, my friend? Or do you toss and turn at night for one reason or ten others? Maybe your minimum wage just can't make it to the end of the month. Maybe you are stuck in a relationship that is killing you and your children. Maybe you've been haunted all your life because you knew you didn't measure up – you weren't as pretty, or smart, or popular, or as fast as your sister or brother.

I know too well what that poor self-image feels like. Growing up I couldn't miss the fact that people turned to take a second look at my sister because of her beauty but they'd stare at me because of my brokenness. If only God had given me an attractive body, or at least a whole one. Living with the sad reality downed me every day of my adolescent years.

Who can calm that turbulent unrest that steals our peace of mind? The Prince of Peace says, "Allow Me." And I answer, *how long, Lord, how long?* The process of becoming comfortable in my own skin took half a century. Meeting *Jehovah Shalom* marked the beginning, but He had many layers of self-condemnation to wade through. Being loved unconditionally by my three daughters helped a lot, but it was a 41st anniversary card from my knight in shining armor, Mr. David Squier, that clinched it. The message conveyed, *You are beautiful just the way you are, regardless of what you do or don't do, even on your not-so-good days, simply because you're you.*

Somehow those words of total acceptance broke through my emotional scars so that my heart heard my lover's love song and dared to peek out of hiding. *You mean I am loveable, stumps and all?* Finally I came to *Shalom's* sweet spot.

Where are you in this long journey to self-acceptance? Jesus Christ, the Prince of Peace wants to be your Knight in Shining Armor. When you say *yes* to His invitation to be His Beloved, He serenades you with this love song: *You are beautiful, just the way I made you. You are perfect. I made no mistakes. And, oh, that part of you that you despise? I'm waiting to meet you there. And I have a gift for you – My gift of Shalom.*

17

Jehovah Mekoddishkem

THE LORD WHO SANCTIFIES

*The Only One Who Can Perfect
Us into a Masterpiece*

*L*oser! *Loser! Loser!* Those were the words that plagued
me from the dawn of my self-awareness. Didn't my missing
legs make me an eyesore? Didn't my disability set me apart
from everyone else? Wasn't I a burden to my family? Feeling
beaten down and alone, I grew up convinced I was the biggest loser on planet earth.

My trek out of loserhood has been the journey of a lifetime. Becoming a Christian was the first step toward silenc-
ing shame. Who can argue with these words? *Even before he
made the world, God loved us and chose us in Christ to be
holy and without fault in his eyes.* (Ephesians 1:4 NLT)

Then came the following heaven-sent truth to bolster
my self worth: *Because of what Christ has done, we have
become gifts to God that he delights in...* (Ephesians 1:11a
TLB) To that I say, *Really, Lord? I'm a gift to You? Could it
be true – You delight in me?*

Little by little God's love penetrated my crusty layers
of self-condemnation as evidenced by this entry in that I

penned in my twenties:

How do I see myself?
In need. Forgetful. Unknowingly straying.
Playing God. Forgiven. His workmanship.
Gaining ground.

Another life-resuscitating revelation came to me in my thirties and I used it to help my little third grade Sunday School girls appreciate their worth. I gain emotional height every time I read it.

I'm Special
No one is more special than me.
No one can increase or decrease my specialness.
It doesn't get bigger or smaller depending on how I feel.
It doesn't get more or less depending on how I act.

It doesn't get taller or shorter
depending on what someone says about me.
I will always walk with my head held high.
I'm special! My Father is a King.

Three steps forward and one back, I've exchanged the lie that I'm a loser for what the Bible says – *We are God's masterpiece.* (Ephesians 2:10a NLT) Translated into everyday language, that verse means *God does not make junk.* My prize plaque containing that kingdom principle was presented to me decades ago by the mother of a speech pathology client with Down syndrome. Kevin Keller's winsome spirit, free of self-condemnation, convinced everyone who knew him of the sanctity of human life. His life provided proof that we are each holy treasures sanctified by God Himself.

Sanctified? For years I strained to understand such a big word. I still didn't get it when a friend, trying to enlighten me, said, "Judy, sanctification simply means set apart for the Master's use." *Huh?* The light bulb of understanding finally went on one Sunday when Ray Stedman, our pastor, said, "Sanctification means God's holiness worked out in our lives, God's righteousness made visible."

A favorite needlework quote

We are made righteous, given right standing with God, the moment we receive Jesus as our Savior. Sanctification, however, is a lifelong process, occurring one day at a time as we read and apply the Bible, as we draw on God's power, and as we allow Jesus Christ to be the Lord of our everything.

Slowly but surely, one step forward, and some days a dozen steps backward, we become like Jesus. By some miracle He becomes visible in us, so when someone spends time with us, they spend time with Him. I experienced this reality recently when my friend Stephanie e-mailed me and said, "So I'll see you next month. I'm eager to be in the presence of Judy and Jesus."

The apostle Paul describes the sanctification process as believers being transformed *from glory to glory*. (II Corinthians 3:18 NASB) But what about days when glory seems like nothing more than a five-letter word? What about days when *from glory to glory* feels more like from icky to slightly better? Or from icky to more icky?

From glory to glory means that God actually reverses the second law of thermodynamics. He cancels entropy – earth's inevitable process of natural decay, which causes everything and everyone to go from good to bad to worse. If God truly can reverse natural decay, it's time for me to replace *Loser, Loser, Loser* with *Jesus loves me this I know for the Bible tells me so.*

No longer need I cower at the Shamer's taunts. I have my new response in place. "Shut thee up, Satan. You don't have a leg to stand on. I'm wrapped in Jesus Christ's robe of righteousness. I'm a saint under construction."

Jehovah Mekoddishkem is relentlessly committed to re-creating each believer into the spittin' image of His Son. And it's for days like that that I keep the life preserver of Philippians 1:6 handy. *There has never been the slightest doubt in my mind that the God who started this great work in you would keep at it and bring it to a flourishing finish on the very day Christ Jesus appears.* (MSG)

One day my old friend Grandpa Gil quoted a favorite

poem he'd memorized to keep him safe from the onslaught of the Shamer. Each year at Joni and Friends Family Retreat, I'd beg, "Please Grandpa Gil, recite the poem again."

How canst Thou love the man I am
and be the God Thou art?
Is darkness to my intellect but sunshine to my heart.
I hear the Accuser roar of all the ills I've done,
I know them all and 1000s more,
Jehovah findeth none.[32]

WHAT ABOUT YOU?

Have you met the Shamer? He's the one who tears you to pieces with deflating accusations. *You'll never amount to anything. You're an embarrassment to the human race. The world would be a better place without you.*

For half a century that old Shamer had me pinned to the mat, until one day I realized shame is pandemic. To confirm my hunch I conducted an informal survey asking random people, "What shames you?"

The first answer came from a man who admitted he'd always felt ashamed that his father was a farmer. Another man, eighty-two years old, expressed shame because of his life-long acne. Then there was the man who came up to me recently after a talk to thank me for mentioning my battle with self-condemnation. He confided that all of his life his family had labeled him a loser.

"Why, pray tell?" I had to ask because I saw nothing that would single him out in a crowd.

"Because of a drooping eyelid," he said with a heavy heart.

One other person, a gal this time, admitted that she had lived with shame because of a defective gene, resulting in an incurable blood disease. I watched as this dear one's simple act of voicing her shame transformed her from the quietest in our Living in the Names of God class to a confident participant. Voicing our shame sets us free.

Surprisingly, all of the above answers came from Christians who deep down know that Jesus loves them. I say to them and I say to myself, didn't Jesus Christ pay a hefty price to once and for all pluck us out of shame's torture chamber? Didn't His crucifixion and resurrection incinerate loserhood once and for all? Didn't He pay the price in full to set us free?

Following his crucifixion and resurrection, Jesus ascended into heaven to sit at the right hand of the Father, interceding for you and interceding for me. When the Shamer attaches *Loser* to our name, Jesus answers – *forgiven, blameless, chosen, royalty, prized possession, beloved.*

The battle rages, but the victory's won. It's time to exchange the Shamer's dagger for *Jehovah Mekoddishkem's* hug. One way to experience that hug is through people who value you and tell you so. Hopefully you have someone like that in your life.

I always felt lavishly loved by my Aunt Helen, who glowed when she said, "My precious Judy, you are beautiful and oh, so special to God and to me." Aunt Helen is safely Home now but she left behind an irrefutable reminder that the Lord's sanctifying work will be accomplished. *The growth of a saint is the task of a lifetime. And we shall be like Him.*

p.s. It won't take long.

Jesus Christ wants to escort us out of the torture chamber into His great throne room, even while we're still on earth. As we behold the radiance of His glory may the roars of the Shamer be drowned out by the angelic and human choirs thundering, "Glory, Glory, Glory."

18

El Olam

THE EVERLASTING GOD

*The God Who Replaces Our
Dead Ends with Life*

I met *El Olam* eyeball to eyeball at Fairfax Nursing Home outside Chicago on a cold wintery weekend as I said my final goodbyes to my champion father. I was forty-four years old. Dad was an old and tired eighty-two. I'd been forewarned that his malignant brain tumor held him hostage most of the time – meaning he might sleep through my visit.

Friday and Saturday I sat by his bedside warmed by decades of father-daughter memories, when suddenly I realized that Dad and I had lived a story that could change the world. God whispered in my ear, *It will.*

As Sunday dawned, I rose early to share a few more hours in Dad's presence before my flight back to California. When I said my last goodbye, my songbird father shot up in bed to sing the winter-of-his-life's final song. With all the strength he could muster, his emboldened words placed me in the eternal, safekeeping of *El Olam.*

Don't be downhearted, look up, look up,

Jesus is on the throne
And He shall supply all your needs from on high
Look up, look up, look up.[33]

33,000 feet high in the sky en route back to San Francisco, heaven filled my thoughts. I thought of Dad's imminent departure from earth, then remembered my Aunt Martha telling me about heaven years earlier. From her open Bible she read John 14:2. *In My Father's house are many dwelling places; if it were not so, I would have told you; for I go to prepare a place for you.* (NASB)

Aunt Martha and I had a unique bond. She had one stump (an amputation due to diabetes) and I had two. I remember her pure white hair. I remember her love for her Bible and her confidence in the promises of God. Fifty years later Aunt Martha resides in one of heaven's mansions and now I have the white hair and the love of my Bible and its promises.

My father, Reverend Rieder, had performed many a memorial service in his lifetime so he knew exactly what he wanted in his. He made sure his favorite violinist played his much-loved Schubert's "Ave Maria" at the beginning and the end of his memorial tribute. He made sure all of his family participated and, of course, the Scripture passage would be his much-loved Psalm 91.

The service flowed without a hitch until the officiating pastor began to read Psalm 90. *Stop everything. Didn't Dad designate Psalm 91, his favorite?* Soon our family realized the Holy Spirit had rewritten the script as we were all comforted by the ageless words of Moses' prayer in Psalm 90:1. *Lord, Thou, hast been our dwelling place in all generations.* (KJV) Moses knew the Lord as his dwelling place as did Father Abraham during his wandering years with no roots to call home. (Abraham's instability literally met the Everlasting God, *El Olam's* stability in chapter 21 of Genesis.)

Becoming a Christ-follower at age twenty meant I became steeped in truths about the eternal God and eternal life in Christ. But only in the last decade have I been confronted with my own mortality. First came the crow's feet by my eyes, then the deep grooves and spreading wrinkles on my face, and most recently the rooster wattle under my chin.

"Er, Er, Er, Er," I crowed one morning. The inevitable decline and entropy of my body is on the march.

That's why my son-in-law Andrew's remark to me the week of my sixty-seventh birthday came as a shocker. There I sat in my wheelchair, donned in my bathrobe, my white hair uncombed and no make up. As Andrew and I sipped our morning cups of coffee, I heard his southern drawl declare, "Miss Judy, you're beautiful."

"Andrew, you're kidding me." His words did not compute.

That's when this Bible-belt boy from Alabama recited from memory Proverbs 31:30. *Charm is deceitful and beauty is vain, But a woman who fears the LORD, she shall be praised.* (NASB)

I'd first heard Proverbs 31 read at my grandma's fu-

Judy and Elisabeth Elliot

neral and at many funerals thereafter, but that was the first time I'd heard it recited for someone still alive, who was feeling anything but beautiful. Thank you, Andrew, for the high honor. Thank you for reprogramming my thinking as you, the next generation's Christ-follower, see me through truth-colored glasses.

As I've dealt with the decline that comes with aging, I remind myself of Elisabeth Elliot's opener for her radio broadcast, Gateway to Joy. I've written her name in the margin of my Bible beside Deuteronomy 33:27: *The eternal God is your refuge, and underneath are the everlasting arms.* (NIV)

As I've pondered what I will be like in my latter years here on earth, I've found my perfect role model, a senior citizen named Mabel, described by John Ortberg in his book *The Life You've Always Wanted.*

The state-run convalescent hospital is not a pleasant place. As I neared the end of the hallway, I saw an old woman strapped up in a wheelchair. Her face was an absolute horror. The empty stare told me she was blind. The large hearing aid over one ear told me that she was almost deaf. One side of her face was eaten by cancer. She drooled constantly. This was Mabel.

Mabel and I became friends and I went to see her once or twice a week. Some days I would read to her from the Bible, and often when I would pause she would continue reciting the passage from memory, word-for-word.

It was not many weeks before I turned from a sense that I was being helpful to a sense of wonder. The question occurred to me, What does Mabel have to think about – hour after hour, day after day, week after week, not even able to know if it's day or night. So I went and asked her, 'Mabel, what do you think about while you lie here?'

And she said, 'I think about Jesus. I think about how good He's been to me. He's all the world to me.' And then Mabel began to sing an old hymn:

Jesus is all the world to me,
My life, my joy, my all.
He is my strength from day to day,
Without Him I would fall.
When I am sad to Him I go,
No other one can cheer me so.
When I am sad He makes me glad.
He's my friend.[34]

Like Mabel, I want to finish in *El Olam's* strength alone. I want people to smell Jesus' cologne over the aroma of my disposable underwear. And I want them to be swept off their feet by Jesus in Judy. So each day I pray, "Lord, You are the Keeper of the Clock. I won't arrive in heaven any sooner or later than You ordain. Until then, please make Your life in me a daily spectacle."

What About You?

Is old age creeping up on you? Any signs of crow's feet or wrinkles that makeup can no longer hide? Any rooster's wattles? Maybe those seem minor to you compared to heart or lung disease, worn out hips or knees, or the painful disfigurement of fingers due to arthritis.

I pass on to you the following poem, which invariably plucks Old Judy out of pending doom to plant her feet on higher ground:

> *I shall not mind the whiteness of my hair*
> *Or that slow steps falter on the stair*
> *Or that young friends hurry as they pass*
> *Or that a strange image greets me in the glass*
> *If I can tell as roots feel in the sod*
> *That I am growing old to bloom before the face of God.*[35]

Are you looking forward to blooming before the face of God? Those of us living with or around disability imagine what it will be like when blind eyes can see and deaf ears can hear. And those of us with mobility issues talk about walking on heaven's streets of gold or leaping like deer. But just last week I heard myself say, "When I get to heaven I want to spend eternity looking at Jesus' nail-scarred feet. My new feet with ten toes will want to thank His for all they suffered to bring me there."

And you, my friend? What do you look forward to doing in heaven? Remember, it's okay if your list is a mile long, because you will have all of eternity to do it. Until then make yourself at home in *El Olam's* everlasting arms. We are heavenbound. Jesus purchased our tickets and He's our personal escort who guarantees our safe arrival. See you there.

19

Goʹel

GOD MY REDEEMER

*The God Who Makes All Things
Beautiful in His Time*

I heard about *Go'el*, the Redeemer God, every Easter when
Dad sang his resurrection solo, "I Know that My Redeemer
Liveth," from Handel's *Messiah*. Dad was God's songbird
until his dying day, never passing up an opportunity to ac-
company a sermon with a solo. Each Easter he publicly reiterated for his congregation and for himself the Redeemer's
promise to make human suffering worthwhile: *As for me, I
know that my Redeemer lives...* (Job 19:25: NASB)

Dad loved Job and quoted him often. I can still hear his
voice reciting Job 23:10 from memory. *But he knoweth the
way that I take: when he hath tried me, I shall come forth
as gold.* (KJV) That's the verse that landed in my gold shoe,
the verse I quote each time I hold up our family's proof that
Go'el, the Redeemer God, liveth.

Easily mistaken for a baby shoe, my gold shoe was once
the orthopedic shoe riveted to the metal stilts I walked on
until I was able to wear artificial limbs at age ten. My boring
brown shoe would not have brought a nickel in a Goodwill

store, but ironically it's the only shoe in the Rieder family that survived the cut; all the rest landed inside the Goodwill donation bin.

I can still picture Dad happening upon my no-longer-used stilts one Saturday while puttering in the garage. Painful memories caught him off guard. *But wait a minute; this daughter's story had a happy ending. Didn't she graduate from college, get married and have a ten-year career as a speech pathologist? And wasn't she pregnant again with his grandchild?* Cancel the hankies; bring on the helium balloons. Down the cellar steps he went to his hobby shop, where he sawed through two rivets. Holding the shoe in his hand, he reached for the can of paint and sprayed the orthopedic shoe gold, proof that God had sprinkled our whole family with gold dust. My champion father was the perfect one to salvage the shoe so that I could tell the world *Go'el's* redemption story.

"Tell me Judy, what will become of your gold shoe when

Judy and granddaughter Brianna   Judy's gold shoe plus Brianna's two

God takes you Home?" my friend Nita posed the question as we were leaving a spring tea where I'd just spoken.

"I don't think anybody will want it, Nita."

Obviously my answer didn't convince her, as she encouraged me to ask my three adult daughters. E-mails went out the next morning: "Anyone interested in Mom's gold shoe down the road?" Naphtalie, our youngest and often our most self-sacrificing daughter, replied that she thought one of the sisters should have it. Emily, our oldest, e-mailed that being the runner in the family, she'd like it. But it was Elizabeth's answer that packed the punch:

> *I want your golden shoe and think I should*
> *get it for the following reasons:*
> *1) Out of your three daughters, I am most*
>   *like you;*
> *2) I am your favorite daughter;*
> *3) I am the shoe queen!*

And wise Elizabeth blessed me with a pair of our granddaughter Brianna's gold shoes to clinch the deal.

I see *Go'el's* footprints all over this one. From an orthopedic shoe came a gold shoe came two gold shoes. From a woman with no legs or feet came three daughters and now three grandbabies with strong legs and feet.

How beautiful on the mountains are the feet of those who bring good news (Isaiah 52:7 NIV) is a verse Kathren Martinez identified as a Judy-verse as we finished our Joni

Saylean, a camper mom, with Judy at
JAF Family Retreat

and Friends Wheels for the World delivery of wheelchairs in Rio de Janeiro in 2008. "God wants me to tell you, you have beautiful feet," she said.

Me? Beautiful feet? I queried, looking down at my legless lap in my wheelchair. How incongruous some would say. *How can a woman with no legs have beautiful feet?* For those of us who have met *Go'el*, the answer comes easily – *because our Redeemer liveth.*

Redeemed means He takes what this old world would throw on the trash heap and sprinkles it with gold dust. He takes humanity's missing pieces and creates Masterpieces. He rescues hopeless cases, bestows them with honor and dignity and actually uses them to bring hope to others.

And the God of the universe makes a house call. He knocks on our heart's door and can't wait to tell us, *Do not fear, for I have redeemed you; I have called you by name; you are Mine!* (Isaiah 43:1b NASB)

Yes, *Go'el* whispers each of our names with an invitation for us to hand over our wounds so that He can bind them. He promises to use them to heal us, to bless us and best of all, to make us a blessing. *Go'el* has big plans for our lives, yours and mine:

I will make all things new, he promised. I will restore what was taken. I will restore your years drooped on crutches and trapped in wheelchairs. I will restore the smiles faded by hurt. I will replay the symphonies unheard by deaf ears and the sunsets unseen by blind eyes. The mute will sing. The poor will feast. The wounds will heal.

I will make all things new. I will restore all things. The child snatched by disease will run to your arms. The freedom lost to oppression will dance in your heart. The peace of a pure heart will be my gift to you.

I will make all things new. New hope. New faith. And most of all new love. The Love of which all other loves speak. The Love before which all other loves pale. The Love you have sought in a thousand ports in a thousand nights...this Love of mine, will be yours.[36]

WHAT ABOUT YOU?

What's your redemption story? Have you allowed *Go'el* to write it? He's waiting for you to admit your need of Him and invite Him to take control of your life: *God, my plans have failed. My dreams are in ashes. I'm too battle-weary to go on. Jesus, I overheard someone say that You died on the cross to rescue me. I'd love for You to do that right now. Thank You in advance for Your miracle.*

Niece Christie's redemption story includes her uncanny vision and insight so that people, like me, look to her as their GPS, event planner and wise counselor, whose sound judgment brings order to this world's chaos. No way would she exchange her God-given spiritual eyes for the physical vision she lacks.

My friend Michele describes herself as a woman who is spiritually alive, though completely paralyzed, dependent on a ventilator, a feeding tube and a catheter. She says she was physically-able sixteen years ago, but spiritually dead. Read her redemption stories at Meetmyfriend.com where she gives testimony to how Jesus sets her free from her daily prison of Lou Gehrig's disease.

And I, the old lady with no legs, can't help but applaud my Redeemer God's holy omission of normal legs and feet in utero. Only He could have turned my orthopedic shoe into our family's golden treasure, containing my life verse. *The affliction you gave me was the best thing that could have happened to me, for it taught me to pay attention to your laws. They are more valuable to be than millions in silver and gold.* (Author's rewording of Psalm 119:71 TLB)

One more question as this book nears the end. Have you found your gold shoe yet? Actually, what God spray paints gold in your life may not be a shoe at all. It may be an empty chair which shouts the absence of a beloved family member. Or an empty womb. Or it may be a medical record crammed with life-threatening diagnoses with yours or a loved one's name on them. Maybe your life has had no successes, only tries.

A gold shoe consists of whatever makes you cringe and drives you to sputter, "I'd be a star with great worth, if only...." But don't dead end there. Hand over the disappointment, the frustration, the fury to *Go'el*, the Redeemer God, so He can make something dazzling and beautiful out of the wasteland of your life. Release the deadbolt and fling open the door of your heart. God wants to personally present you with *bouquets of roses instead of ashes, messages of joy instead of news of doom and a praising heart instead of a languid spirit.* (Isaiah 61:3 MSG)

20

A Review

LIVING DAILY
IN THE NAMES OF GOD

Sitting at my pastor father's feet Sunday after Sunday growing up, hearing him finish a sermon with a song, I was destined to become a songbird. No church solos from this girl's one octave range, but I sound great at the Y. As I sing my heart out, the other seniors in the women's dressing room think I do opera after my swim. Deep down I know the truth – I sing because God gave me a song.

Granted, there are seasons when our song dies. Mine sure did as a mother without legs waking up to the day's demands and realizing, "It's a *legs job*!" Post-partum depression stifled my song soon after the arrival of our third daughter.

I still have the pin Dad gave me during those bleak months. The inscription, *He is Our Song*, took the pressure off. And it proved true. Jesus serenaded me with the song I could sing no more as I was stretched beyond my human capacity, flattened and exhausted. I missed it at first, but gradually, faintly, His song broke through. His song promised unlimited resources to replace my infinite inadequacies. His song brought approval, not condemnation. His song warmed my cold feet.

Yes, God Himself is the song when the music goes out of our lives. That's one of the reasons I fell in love with eighteen of His Hebrew names. Each name has sung a unique love song from God's heart to mine.

ELOHIM:
Remember I created you and have big plans for your life.

EL ELYON:
Feeling low? Allow Me to be your high.

JEHOVAH:
Whatever you need today, I AM.

JEHOVAH RAAH:
Nestle in, little lamb. You're safe with me,
your Good Shepherd.

JEHOVAH SHAMMAH:
Feeling alone? You can't go anywhere that
I'm not already there.

EL ROI:
Your pain is My pain.
Be comforted knowing that I removed pain's
stinger on the cross.

JEHOVAH NISSI:
The battle is already won.
Trust Me and raise the victory flag.
JEHOVAH TSIDKENU:
Allow Me to wipe your smudged slate clean.

EL SHADDAI:
Trade in all your insufficiencies for My All-Sufficiencies.

EL GIBBOR:
Allow Me to save the day.

JEHOVAH JIREH:
My more-than-enough exceeds your never-enough.

ADONAI:
Are you ready to hand over your life so I can bless you?

ADONAI TSURI:
Allow Me to be your rock-solid stability in life's squalls.

JEHOVAH RAPHA:
I'm with you in your broken places.
Watch Me use them to heal you.

JEHOVAH SHALOM:
Experience My peace that guarantees
smooth sailing in every storm.

JEHOVAH MEKODDISHKEM:
Believe Me. My work in you will be a WOW!

EL OLAM:
Fret not. You are heaven-bound and in
Me you can enjoy it now.

GO'EL:
My Specialty is transforming your wastelands
into worshipful wonderlands.

Blessed is the day when we wake up and hear God singing His love song with our name in it. Mind you, it's the song that He's sung from the beginning of time, but for most of us self-effort, pleasures and successes have drowned it out. Interesting how too often we hear it for the first time in our pits of despair, our prisons of fear and graveyards of grief.

For a moment the song's message sounds too good to be true, and we question. *You love me, even though? You have big plans for little old me? You can bring shalom to the craziness? I'm forgivable? You want to stuff me to the full with Your adequacy so that I'll never come up short? You want to take all of my losses and make me a winner?*

Suddenly willing, we say *yes* to the Singer. We accept His embrace and, over time, embrace Him back until one day we become able to embrace ourselves. As our voice joins His, we enter the glorious choir of the ages and even become willing to accept the embrace of others.

Pastor Bob kneeling by Judy

I felt Jesus' embrace recently during the Sunday morning worship service. As the congregation spontaneously rose from their seats during the singing of Stand Up, Stand Up for Jesus, our pastor, Bob Bonner, walked over and knelt down beside my wheelchair. My brokenness felt heaven and earth's embrace so that my always-seated-posture stood tall. His joining my inability to participate plucked me from the humiliating back tier to the seat of honor for me, God's beloved in the glorious choir of the ages.

I keep hearing my one octave range returning to an old hymn, which I call my tribute to the God whose greatness requires many names. Actually, I want to sing it from the urn holding my ashes at my memorial service, and I want to sing it when I cartwheel through the open gates of heaven. Leaving no room for error, I want heaven's and earth's standing ovations to be directed to Jesus, the One who created with no mistakes and companioned with me from the womb to the tomb.

Some day life's journey will be o'er.
And I shall reach that distant shore;

I'll sing while ent'ring heaven's door,
"Jesus led me all the way."

Chorus:
Jesus led me all the way,
Led me step by step each day;
I will tell the saints and angels as I lay
My burdens down,
"Jesus led me all the way."[37]

What About You?

Have you said *yes* to the Singer? Have you accepted God's embrace yet? My prayer is that as you complete this book you are beginning a new chapter in your relationship with our God, who longs to be known on a first name basis. Not only is He knowable, He created you with a plan for your life, which He can author and finish when you relinquish your control to His.

Maybe you are saying, "Life has worn me down; my fairy tale expectations have become nightmares. I have no more energy and just have to abort the mission."

Despairing as those remarks may seem, they can be the actual launching pad for the collaborative connection between you and the God who created you to be in an intimate relationship with Himself.

Remember how my love affair with the God-who-has-many- names began? My world was caving in when I sputtered, "God, this is too BIG! I'll take all the help You can muster. Send the troops." Quite a demeaning remark to the Power Source of the universe, but rather than be insulted, eighteen aspects of His Personhood showed up on my doorstep, becoming my lifeline. His Majesty and me, we became a team.

I pray His Majesty and you begin writing stories of your own – accounts of how you've seen Him, how He's rescued you, how He's equipped you and how He's healed you so that you can become His healing agent in our hurting world.

As your eyes open more and more to His presence, be prepared to hear yourself make remarks like: *Thanks, Jehovah Rapha, for Your healing touch during last night's family strife; Bless You, El Roi, for seeing my pain and companioning with me when I was overlooked for the promotion at work; and Go'el, My Redeemer, my hope is in You alone as I hand over my shattered dreams and broken life.* I add, "Keep it coming! Such comments are proof that your theology is becoming autobiography – proof of your growing understanding of who God is and who He wants to be in your life."

Growing up with benedictions, I choose Jeremiah 29:11-13 as my closing *good words*. Remember that Jeremiah 29:11 is the verse God's Spirit whispered to my aching parents the first year of my life. Step by step, we watched His promise become reality, and though the road was difficult, we are all thankful we didn't quit before God's happy ending.

Draw on the limitless resources of His many names as you wait for His promise to ring true in your life and as you march forth into His happy ending. *"For I know the plans I have for you," declares the Lord, "plans to prosper you and not to harm you, plans to give you hope and a future. Then you will call on me and come and pray to me, and I will lis-*

ten to you. You will seek me and find me when you seek me with all your heart..." (Jeremiah 29:11-13 NIV)

21

Last Word

GIVING THANKS FOR
THE GIFT OF MY LIFE

Looking back, I can remember the moment in time when I, an ungrateful teenager, scowled at my mother's comment, "Judy, someday you'll appreciate your Christian heritage." Those were wilderness years, but Mom's God met me, thanks to my wasteland, and proved her right.

And now I say, "Mom, I hope your feet are stomping for joy in the Hebrews 11 grandstands of faith as you see your Christian legacy alive in me and now alive in your grand-daughters – Emily, Elizabeth and Naphtalie, and even in your great-granddaughter Brianna Cole." I know my stumps were stompin' for joy the Sunday I listened to Emily give the following speech at church:

> "She's going to live, I'm sorry to say," were the words of the obstetrician when a tiny, helpless baby was born. Something was ab-normal about this screaming child. She had incomplete legs and a deformed hand. The obstetrician knew that babies like this were just put on this earth for trouble and extra

work. Her parents loved her strongly, and they would make sure that she got many things that most little girls get.

But would this child be worth all the effort and extra money to raise her, not to mention the inconvenience? What did God have in store for this young girl who would learn to walk on artificial limbs?

Through her growing years she learned to trust a God "who makes no mistakes." At age thirteen she began giving speeches about how God put so much value into her life. She quoted Psalm 139:15-16, which says, *You were there God, when I was being formed in utter seclusion. You saw me before I was born, and scheduled each day of my life before I began to breathe.* (TLB)

She talked about how God had a plan for her life, and she talked about the sanctity of human life. She spoke the truth that God has a plan for each and every baby that is formed in their mother's womb, and it is not an accident to be born with a disability.

If this woman were born today, with modern medical science, the doctors would have known ahead of time that she was disabled. There would have been a much higher chance she would have been aborted. If she had been aborted, then I wouldn't be here today, because she is my mother.

My mother is one of the most important people in my life and in many others. Because of her strong faith in God, she has reached out and touched so many lives with her amazing stories of how God works – how He changed her pain and suffering as a child into glory and happiness as an adult.

Every single person on this earth was put in this world for a purpose. Each life is sacred and specially made by God. My mother has proven that. Even though she was born with less than most, she can still be all that she can be, which is a lot."

To this day, I marvel how a mom without legs could give birth to daughters whose legs were not only healthy, but strong enough to help their mom succeed at the *legs job* called motherhood. And how great my joy to see these girls, now adults, join the glorious choir of the ages as they speak out about the value of every human life.

Daughter Naphtalie wrote the following in a Value Paper at the University of Oregon:

> "I have been blessed with the opportunity of being raised by a mom with a disability. My mom, Judy Squier, was born without legs, and since then she has struggled to overcome the obstacles set in her path because of her handicap. However, it is because of my mom's disability that she is a strong individual who has proved to the world that disabilities are not the end of the world. They are merely stepping stones for God to show his power in our weakness."

Yes, Naphtalie, shout it from the rooftop! Disability is not the end of the world, but merely a stepping stone to God. Ironically, He's able to heal us all through the wounds of a few. He knows that brokenness is where He can get His foot in the door in the lives of a people who crave human strength, self-reliance and our own agenda.

Brokenness is His *modus operandi* to stop us in our tracks and to convince us we can't do one nanosecond of this life on our own. Meanwhile, His *magnum opus*, His Masterpiece is on hold while He waits outside the thistle-covered door of our hearts as we try at all costs to fix, patch, mend, or restore what's broken. And finally, if it can't be fixed, we dispose of it. Sadly, we have become a disposable generation.

Years ago I volunteered at a local pregnancy center. As I attended the training sessions and read the books to become a counselor, I was horrified to discover the *accepted* seek-and- destroy mentality in hospitals across the country. *You mean abortions are performed on babies like me – just because they're missing limbs? A life is destroyed because of a hole in the spine? Oh no, not the precious babies with Down syndrome.* That's when it hit me. *I am a member of an endangered species! But wait a minute, I can be a voice for those who have no voice, my brothers and sisters in brokenness. Lord, use me.*

Amniocentesis is our modern medical procedure to identify and often eliminate babies with genetic and/or physical abnormalities. Ultrasound machines are invaluable for determining due date, but they are also used to determine the viability of the unborn.

The world says: They're bad, abort.
GOD SAYS: I INVENTED LIFE AND CALL IT SACRED.

The world says: It's hopeless.
GOD SAYS: MY SPECIALTY IS HOPELESS CASES.

The world says: It will be the death of you.
GOD SAYS: IT WILL BE THE LIFE OF YOU.

Given modern medical procedures, the utter seclusion of the womb is being invaded and man is making the decision to accept or reject the life within. Aborting babies with birth defects is now an acceptable practice across America and around the world.

Heartbreaking was the moment I realized:

If my birth defect and I were conceived
in this day and age,
Given medical technology's ability
to identify imperfections,
Given the world's mindset to eliminate broken babies,
And given the physician's counsel that ending these lives
would be the kind thing to do –

If I were conceived in this day and age,
My song may well have been silenced,
And my story would read as follows

_____

_____

_____

_____

_____

_____*!*

End Notes

1   Kay Arthur, *Lord, I Want to Know You* (New Jersey, Fleming H. Revell Company, 1984).

2   Tim Hansel, *You Gotta Keep Dancin'* (Elgin, Illinois, David C. Cook Publishing, 1985), p.41.

3   Edward Caswall (translator), *When Morning Gilds the Sky*, Public Domain.

4   Holman Hunt (artist), *The Light of the World*, 1851, {{PD-US}} Public Domain.

5   Nicholson & Lee,eds., *The Oxford Book of English Mystical Verse*, Elizabeth Barrett Browning #86 *Aurora Leigh: Earth's Crammed with Heaven* (New York: Bartleby.com, 2000).

6   Robert G. Kemper, *An Elephant's Ballet* (New York: The Seabury Press, 1977).

7   St Patrick, *Christ Be with Me, Hymns for the Family of God* (Nashville: Paragon Associates, Inc., 1976), 643.

8   Brother Lawrence, *Practicing the Presence of God* (New York: Doubleday, 1977).

9   Caroline Alexander, *The Endurance: Shackleton's Legendary Antarctic Expedition* (New York: Alfred A. Knopf, 2001), 165.

10 Sarah Young, *Introduction to Jesus Calling* (Nashville: Thomas Nelson, 2008).

11 *Hagar and the Angel in the Desert*, © 1896-1902, by James Jacques Joseph Tissot {{PD-US}} Public Domain.

12 Used by permission from Joni Eareckson Tada, Joni and

Friends International Disability Center, All rights reserved.

13 Sabine Baring-Gould, *Onward Christian Soldiers*, Public Domain.

14 Ira Wilson, *Make Me a Blessing*, Public Domain.

15 John Emms (artist), *St. Bernards to the Rescue*, {{PD-US}} Public Domain.

16 Noelle Brun, *Famous Animals in History and Legend* (New York: The Lion Press, 1968), 50.

17 Brennan Manning, *Abba's Child* (Colorado Springs: Nav-Press, 2002), 13.

18 John T. Grape, *Jesus Paid it All*, Public Domain.

19 Laurent de La Hire: *Le Sacrifice d'Abraham*, 1650 (Musée des beaux-arts de Reims).

20 Cover Art for *Riches for Romania* by Fernan Fernandez.

21 Erik Weihenmayer, *Touch the Top of the World* (USA: Penguin Group, 2002).

22 Johnson Oatman, Jr., *Higher Ground*, Public Domain.

23 Charles Wesley, *And Can It Be?* Public Domain.

24 Oswald Chambers, *My Utmost for His Highest*, December 9 (New York: Dodd, Mead & Company, 1966), 344.

25 Used by permission from Grace Rhie, *My Adonai*, All rights reserved.

26 Mrs. Charles Cowman, *Streams in the Desert*, November 4 (Grand Rapids: Zondervan Publishing House, 1965), 320.

27 Joni Eareckson Tada, *More Precious than Silver*, July 1 (Grand Rapids: Zondervan Publishing House, 1998).

28 Edward Mote, *The Solid Rock*, Public Domain.

29 Used by permission from Hart Classic Editions, Nathan Greene's *The Comforter*, Copyright © 1996, All rights reserved.

30 Elizabeth Cheney, *Overheard in the Garden, Streams in the Desert*, October 10 (Grand Rapids: Zondervan Publishing House, 1965), 294.

31 Horatio Spafford, *It is Well with My Soul*, Public Domain.

32 Wade Ebersole, *How Canst Thou Love*, New Tribe missionary, Papua, New Guinea.

33 Author Unknown, *Don't Be Downhearted*.

34 Taken from *The Life You've Always Wanted* by John Ortberg. Copyright © 2002 by Zondervan. Used by permission of Zondervan.

35 Author Unknown, *I Shall Not Mind*.

36 Reprinted by permission. *When God Whispers Your Name*, Max Lucado, 1994, Thomas Nelson Inc. Nashville, Tennessee, All rights reserved.

37 © 1954 John W. Peterson Music Company. *Jesus Led Me All the Way*. All rights reserved. Used by permission.

ALSO BY JUDY SQUIER

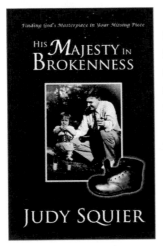

HIS MAJESTY IN BROKENNESS

Big or small, missing pieces can break the best of us. Who doesn't want to escape life's brokenness that weakens and disables us? Or does it? Unable to run from her birth defect, Judy's life became a stage for God to show up and craft a masterpiece out of her detested missing pieces. Be fortified and set free as you encounter Judy's authentic responses to daily struggles. May you, like she, discover the One who makes suffering worth all the pain.

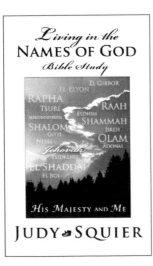

LIVING IN THE NAMES OF GOD BIBLE STUDY

Is it possible to know the God of the universe on a first name basis? You betcha. Allow Judy Squier to walk you through a *Living in the Names of God Bible Study* focusing on eighteen of God's Hebrew names — names that not only help you understand who He is, but help you understand who you are. Join the study and join the Lovers of His Names chorus as — *All day we parade God's praise — we thank you by name over and over.* (Psalm 44:8 MSG)

Available at:
WWW.JUDYSQUIER.COM